T0335056

The Sociology of Literature

The Sociology of Literature

GISÈLE SAPIRO

Translated by Madeline Bedecarré and Ben Libman

STANFORD UNIVERSITY PRESS
Stanford, California

Stanford University Press
Stanford, California

English translation © 2023 by the Board of Trustees of the Leland Stanford Junior University. All rights reserved.

The Sociology of Literature was originally published in French in 2014 under the title *La sociologie de la littérature,* © Éditions La Découverte, Paris, 2014.

Preface and translators' note © 2023 by the Board of Trustees of the Leland Stanford Junior University. All rights reserved.

No part of this book may be reproduced or transmitted in any form or by any means, electronic or mechanical, including photocopying and recording, or in any information storage or retrieval system, without the prior written permission of Stanford University Press.

Printed and bound by CPI Group (UK) Ltd, Croydon, CR0 4YY

Library of Congress Cataloging-in-Publication Data
Names: Sapiro, Gisèle, author.
Title: The sociology of literature / Gisèle Sapiro ; translated by
    Madeline Bedecarré and Ben Libman.
Other titles: Sociologie de la littérature. English
Description: Stanford, California : Stanford University Press, 2023. |
    "Originally published in French in 2014 under the title La sociologie
    de la littérature." | Includes bibliographical references and index.
Identifiers: LCCN 2023009017 (print) | LCCN 2023009018 (ebook) |
    ISBN 9781503633179 (cloth) | ISBN 9781503637597 (paperback) |
    ISBN 9781503637603 (ebook)
Subjects: LCSH: Literature and society.
Classification: LCC PN51 .S3125 2023 (print) | LCC PN51 (ebook) |
    DDC 306.4/2--dc23/eng/20230607
LC record available at https://lccn.loc.gov/2023009017
LC ebook record available at https://lccn.loc.gov/2023009018

Cover design: Jason Anscomb
Typeset by Elliott Beard in Miller Text 10.5/15

To my students

Contents

Contents

Translators' Note

To grasp the full import of this book, one need only begin at the beginning, with Gisèle Sapiro's dedication: *À mes étudiants* (To my students). This is a book for students of research, whether they be found in doctoral programs or in faculty positions with decades of tenure behind them. Sapiro, like her mentor Pierre Bourdieu, takes very seriously the task of combining multiple roles that, for many, are nonjoinable: the pedagogue, scholar, and public intellectual. Her stature in France as an authority and frequent commentator on cultural politics has not kept her from the classroom. If Sapiro's byline is often encountered in the pages of *Le Monde*, *L'Humanité*, *Libération*, and *AOC (Analyse Opinion Critique)*, she herself is usually found among her students, each of whom is working to deepen the discipline she has so fiercely championed for more than two decades. We see this book as belonging in the classroom as well; it is just as much a document for pedagogy as it is a tool and resource for research.

In France, where the sociology of literature took root, the present text is a crystallization of methods, histories, and approaches that, to one degree or another, will be familiar to sociologists and literary critics alike; it offers a program for further understanding and pursuing a discipline whose merits have long been proven in that country. For readers from the English-speaking world, we hope that *The Sociology of Literature* will open up broad new avenues for research and intellectual experimentation. That *La Sociologie de la littérature* (2014) was originally published in the "Repères" series at La Découverte speaks to the esteem in which this branch of sociology is held in France. The aim of the "Repères" collection is to offer rigorous, clear, and accessible introductions to the most important disciplines and subdisciplines in the sciences, each volume being no longer than 128 pages, costing no more than 11 euros, and taking the form of a pocket book. That everything one needs to know about the sociology of literature might be found in one's coat pocket alongside, say, everything one needs to know about economics is evidence of the discipline's hard-won institutionalization in France.

In the United States, the story is rather different. The sociology of literature has thus far made its deepest inroads in literary studies. Following the publication of Bourdieu's *The Rules of Art* (1996) in English, American literary critics, long accustomed to borrowing methods from other disciplines for productive use in their own, found a new wealth of possibilities in what has since become a landmark text in the humanities. There is an incongruity here that can only be attributed to the peculiar transformations that attend what Bourdieu called "the international circulation of ideas": in France, the sociology of literature is resolutely a branch of sociology, not literary studies—and Sapiro herself is undeniably seen more as a sociologist than as a literary scholar. The same went for Bourdieu. This is not, however, to scold American readers for mistaking the contents of this book and others like it as being fit for "the wrong" discipline. Quite the contrary: in their idiosyncratic American reception, the sociologists of literature have discovered new freedoms and possibilities of their own, realizing that here, perhaps more than in France, they have an opportunity to rub shoulders with literary criticism and engage in interdisciplinary dialogue with its practitioners.

It was therefore our aim, in translating this book, to offer American literary critics and sociologists alike a foundational text—a handbook—upon which to base their future research and collaborations. *The Sociology of Literature*, then, is presented here not so much as an intervention as a rallying point, where scholars from varying fields can take stock of and rearticulate the work they have already been doing, and can borrow the tools and principles that might help them push ahead.

The Sociology of Literature is also offered as a kind of reset to what has, until now, often been a contentious (if sometimes ill-informed) debate around the sociology of literature in the American academic context. Most commonly, the sociological approach to literary study has been criticized by literary scholars for reducing texts to their social environments, and by sociologists for privileging an elite and unuseful object of study. As will be clear to the reader of this book, neither of these critiques is an accurate assessment of the sociology of literature. As with any interdisciplinary effort, the challenges of bringing the sociological perspective to bear upon literary study—or the literary perspective to bear upon sociology—should not be taken lightly. But thanks to Sapiro's work, we now know what tools to wield and what paths to explore.

The challenges of translating this volume have been both interesting and numerous. Most important to us was to effect a certain continuity with the better known books on the sociology of literature already published in English. Thus, whereas Bourdieu's term *l'espace des possibles* entered the English lexicon almost three decades ago as "the space of possibles," we have retained this translation—even as we might, in another reception context, have gone with "space of possibilities." Certain terms that might jar or startle as somewhat foreign-sounding (e.g., the use of "consecration" in the context of awarding a literary prize) have been retained for that very reason: Sapiro, who worked closely with us on this translation, wanted readers to pause over the words and phrases that convey the most important concepts in the sociology of culture. Other decisions were exacting for reasons unrelated to the business of finding *le mot juste.* Although some have called into question the appropriateness of the term "field," given its connotative associations with the historical practice of slavery, we have preserved it precisely because, in borrowing the term as a metaphor for his own sociological theory, Bourdieu had in mind another sort of field entirely: the magnetic field, rife with charges, currents, and vectors—a perfect image of the dynamic social arrangement he set out to describe.

Above all, we have tried to preserve the clarity and grace of the original text for you, the reader, a student much like ourselves.

Madeline Bedecarré

Ben Libman

Preface

The Black Lives Matter and #MeToo movements have brought the question of the complex relationship between representation and reality back to the center of public debate. Literature is a cultural form that can either convey existing representations, including racist, classist, sexist, and transphobic ones—and those peddling the hierarchization of legitimate identities and all other forms of social disqualification—or else subvert them. Literature is in this sense a site for the reproduction or subversion of symbolic violence, understood as a form of violence that is masked because euphemized, and which thus contributes to reproducing forms of domination by inculcating them as natural, and therefore legitimate, among the dominated (Bourdieu 2002b). This power proper to literature, as to other cultural forms, makes it not only an object of worship and a source for exegesis, but also the object of symbolic struggles, censorship, lawsuits, boycotts, and cancellations. Yet traditional literary studies, especially in

---

This preface was written by the author specially for the English-language edition.

the wake of New Criticism and structuralism, have tended to focus on the text and its specific forms. The sociology of literature does not reduce literature to representations of the social world, but instead apprehends literature in its different modes of social existence, from its most materialized forms (the book as object) to its cognitive dimensions, and through its development into literary genres, its classification in aesthetic currents, its appropriations by political movements, and so on.

It is surprising that in the United States, where consciousness of the power of cultural forms has been sharpened by feminist, queer, and antiracist movements, the sociology of literature remains so marginal. This is no doubt due to disciplinary compartmentalization, exacerbated by the separation of the humanities from the social sciences, as well as to the lack of interest in literature among sociologists, and in sociology among literary scholars. There are certainly deeper reasons why this state of affairs is not specific to the English-speaking world, like the fact that literary scholars fear a sacrilegious sociological reductionism, which reminds them of Marxism, and that literature can be seen as a futile or elitist object in the eyes of sociologists. (I myself was trained in literary theory and philosophy, but I discovered sociology, then a somewhat scorned discipline, only belatedly through Pierre Bourdieu's sociology of literature, and subsequently became a sociologist.) These reasons have very old origins, outlined in the first chapter of this book. The purpose of the book, however, is to illustrate all the benefits that both disciplines stand to gain from the intermingling of their approaches and lines of questioning.

Published in 2014 as part of La Découverte's "Repères" collection, the remit of which is to take stock of a research domain and propose new directions for it (the collection is aimed primarily at students, but also at researchers engaging in the discipline), this book was initially intended for a French-speaking audience, and was based on a predominantly French-language corpus and on examples of research conducted for the most part in the French-speaking world (including work by researchers from other countries). Although the format of the collection severely limited the breadth of references I could cite, this did not amount to a major distortion of the subject matter, because it is mainly in the French linguistic space that the sociology of literature has, since its latest upsurge in the 1970s, evolved. Moreover, the examples aim above all to open up avenues of research that can be transposed to other sociocultural contexts, laying the foundations for a comparative approach that, as Bourdieu says, can only be carried out "from system to system" (Bourdieu 1991a: 630–31). This book has so far been translated into Spanish, Portuguese, Japanese, Turkish, and Bulgarian, and it serves—in South America in particular, but also elsewhere (in Germany, for instance)—as a reference, along with Bourdieu's *The Rules of Art* and Pascale Casanova's *The World Republic of Letters*, for the development of research in this domain.

In the English-speaking world, where work has long been done on the history of censorship and the social construction of authorship in the wake of Foucault (1999), and where queer theory and feminist and postcolonial studies have drawn attention to the gendered and racialized aspects of cultural works, there has recently been a growing interest in other objects of study in the sociology of literature, such as creative writing programs, literary agents, the editorial process, translation, reading clubs, and literary festivals. This is why the English-language edition of this book is an expanded edition, taking into account as much as possible these recent developments, with an updated bibliography, mainly in English and French, in the hope that it can contribute to the flourishing of the field.

I concluded my last book, *Peut-on dissocier l'œuvre de l'auteur ?* (*Can We Separate the Work from the Author?* [Sapiro

2020b]), by writing that while boycotting is a right, analysis is nevertheless preferable to erasure, because the erasure of a work, especially in the case of the classics, risks wiping out the traces of symbolic violence along with it, and so generating a collective amnesia. By contrast, the sociology of literature can be a tool for anamnesis of this symbolic violence and the role that literary works may have had in its reproduction or subversion.

Gisèle Sapiro

PARIS

February 6, 2023

Introduction

The sociology of literature approaches literature as a social fact. This entails a two-pronged examination: the study of literature as a social phenomenon, in which a great number of institutions and individuals who produce, consume, and judge literary texts participate; and the study of how time periods and social issues are represented in literary texts.

This seemingly simple proposition raises a number of questions. What defines an authoritative text? A work as it was published by its author? But in this case, what to make of Kafka's works published by Max Brod after his death? or of different versions of a text published by an author? or of variations found in manuscripts? Should we focus on the genesis of a text and understand it, like Sartre, as part of a larger "creative project"? or, otherwise, on its interpretation, which can vary depending on the readers and the time period?

Indeed, the meaning of a literary text or of any cultural production cannot be reduced to the author's intent. Apart from the fact that authors are not always conscious of what they do, the meaning of the work depends on two factors that elude the cre-

1

ator. First, the meaning of a work resides not merely in its internal construction, as hermeneutic criticism claims, but also in a national or international space of possibles (as defined by Bourdieu),[1] the contours of which are traced by the totality of symbolic productions, present and past, among which it is situated at the time of its publication or republication. The singular work thus defines itself through its relationship to other cultural productions in terms of themes, genres, composition, and devices. The literary work is a vehicle for representations of the social world, which can be more or less shared by contemporaries (depending on the social group: class, gender, nation, ethnic group, and so on) and can be found in nonliterary texts. Which leads us to the question that specifically concerns us here: what is the relevant context for understanding a work of literature? Is it the author's unique biography, which Sartre prioritized in his study of Flaubert, the social group (or class) which the author originally hails from or belongs to, or the social characteristics of the reading public? Is the relevant context to be found in national literature, on which literary history was based, or in world literature (Goethe's *Weltliteratur*)? Which is more important: the social conditions of production and circulation of literary works, as contended by the founders of cultural studies? or the categories of understanding of the culture to which the work belongs, following the neo-Kantian tradition from Cassirer to Panofsky?

The second factor concerns the appropriations and uses that are made of a text, the meaning it is given, and the attempts at annexation to which it is subjected. These processes of reception are not external to the history of literary production. First, the reception of a work of literature has effects not only on its social meaning, but also on its position in the hierarchy of symbolic goods, which is assigned by its critical reception, its distribution in bookstores (for instance, placement in displays or position on bestseller lists), and so on. Second, the reception of literary works often has effects on authors themselves, who can be led to change or adjust their "creative project" depending on the reactions and expectations provoked by this reception. Third, the (re)appropriations of literary works from the past, or from other cultures, are at the very heart of the mechanisms of reproduction or renewal of the space of literary possibles: Lautréamont was exhumed by the Surrealists in opposition to writers of their time, Dos Passos and Faulkner were anointed in France by Sartre against the classic novelistic forms from the nineteenth century, and Flaubert was annexed by the Nouveau Roman in a coup against committed literature. This handful of examples alone confirms the role reappropriations play in the history of literature.

Like many areas of specialization (for example, the sociology of law), the sociology of literature is torn between two disciplines. But it also suffers from the long history of tensions and frictions between sociology and literary studies: the former established itself as a discipline by breaking away from the humanist culture that prevailed at the end of the nineteenth century, while the latter remains hostile to any "deterministic" approach to literature.[2] Indeed, the sociology of literature had to overcome a resistance, on the part of literary scholars, to objectification stemming from the belief in the indeterminate and unique nature of literary works. Too "sociological" for literary scholars and too "literary" for sociologists, affiliated in some countries with literature, and in others with sociology, this subdiscipline suffers from a lack of institutionalization that contrasts with the richness of the work produced in the field for half a century. The dialogue initiated between literary scholars and sociologists, which strives to rise above disciplinary tensions, opens up promising channels of collaboration that this book hopes to encourage (see Desan et al. 1988; Baudorre, Rabaté, and Viart 2007).

This book aims to provide an overview of the current advancements in this growing field, by placing an emphasis on the sociological angle and on methodology (including quantitative methods, such as multiple correspondence analysis and network analysis), as well as on intersections with the questions posed by the sociology of art, culture, mass media, publishing, translation, professions, social relations (class, gender, and race), globalization, and so forth, into which this approach can offer insight.[3] In constant dialogue with historians of literature (Lyon-Caen and Ribard 2010), this overview also points to possibilities for cross-fertilization with gender studies and postcolonial studies.

The first chapter sketches the history of this specialty and the theories that most shaped it, in particular those that attempted to transcend the division between internal and external analyses of texts. To this end, the sociological approach to literature is conceived of as the study of mediations between literary works and the social conditions of their production. These mediations are situated across three axes opening up areas of research that are examined in the following chapters: first, the material conditions of the production of literary works, as well as the mode of operation of the world of letters; second, the sociology of works (*sociologie des oeuvres*), from the representations that they convey to the modalities of their production by their authors; third, the conditions of their reception and appropriation, as well as the uses that are made of them.

Drawing on examples from empirical studies, chapters II through IV will also discuss the methods deployed to address the questions raised. In addition to the qualitative methods traditionally utilized to study the literary fact (documentary analysis, study of the content of literary works and criticism), a sociological approach relies on studies of individual trajectories, which differ from biography, as well as on interviews and ethnographic observation for contemporary objects of study. But it is above all through quantitative methods that the sociology of literature differentiates itself from traditional literary approaches. Despite the common representation of the creative act as unique, there is no dearth of quantifiable or measurable aspects in the processes of the production and reception of literature: the social characteristics of authors and reading publics, types of publications, publishing formats, genres, networks of relationships, and so on. Whether by way of a prosopography (collective biography) of a group of writers, network analysis, lexicometrical analysis (which is now gaining traction in literary studies along with digital text analysis),[4] or studies about reading, quantitative approaches shed light on seemingly irreducible facets of literary trajectories, literary texts, or reading experiences in a given social configuration, provided that they draw on more astute qualitative analyses. The book will also examine the perspectives opened up by the denationalization of literary history, such as studies on the transnational circulation of works of literature (especially through translation, but also through imitation) and on migratory trajectories (the effects of exile on artistic creation).

I

Sociological Theories and Approaches to Literature

The relationship between literature and sociology has always been a contentious and competitive one, but also one characterized by exchange and cross-fertilization. Literature is invested in social life, which it portrays under various aspects. From Balzac's and Flaubert's sweeping social frescos to Zola and his school's naturalist studies of social milieu, since the end of the eighteenth century the realist tradition has described the mores of different social spheres (from the aristocracy and the bourgeoisie to the underbelly of society) and professional ones (journalism, medicine, the stock market, and so on); and it has probed institutions like marriage, the family, and the school, as well as societal transformations and the dynamics of social mobility (upward and downward). Yet the specialization of sociology as a science and its institutionalization as an academic discipline at the end of the nineteenth century stripped writers of one of their areas of expertise, especially as the "moral science of manners" asserted itself by breaking with literary culture (Lepenies 1988; Heilbron 2006; Sapiro 2004a). The sociology of art became at this time a domain of sociology, but it was not until the second half of the twentieth century that the sociology of literature emerged as a specialty. The sociology of literature was at first part of literary studies, before also becoming a subfield within the discipline of sociology.

Diametrically opposed to the belief in the social indeterminacy of artworks—a product of the Romantic ideology of the "uncreated creator" (Bourdieu 1993, 139)—as well as to formalist or purely textual approaches to literature, the sociology of literature considers literature to be a social activity that depends on conditions of production and circulation, and sees it as something closely linked to values and a "worldview." The sociology of literature therefore calls for the study of the relationships between the text and its context, which, in terms of methodology, poses the problem of the tension between internal and external analysis, the former being interested in the structure of literary works, while the latter underscores their social function. Attempts to transcend this division have focused on the mediations between a work of literature and its conditions of production.

After providing a brief overview of the "protosociological" theories of literature, which tried to identify the laws of literary history, I will discuss the main sociological theories and approaches to literature that have been devised since the 1960s: Marxist reflection theory, cultural studies, the sociology of the book and of reading, field theory, the theory of literary institutions, polysystem theory, symbolic interactionism (art worlds), network analysis, and "distant reading."

Literature as Social Fact

"Protosociological" analyses of literature were primarily concerned with its social effects. In the eighteenth century, studies on the social dimension of the literary world began to be published. The postrevolutionary conjuncture prompted reflections upon the social and political roles proper to men and women of letters. When penned by Madame de Staël, such reflections took the form of a comparison of the historical development of national literatures in order to delineate their laws. This approach, developed in the mid-nineteenth century by Hippolyte Taine, went on to found the basis of the literary history that Gustave Lanson established as an academic discipline at the end of the century by rooting it more solidly within history and sociology.

The Social Effects of Literature

The ancient theory of imitation, which Plato developed in *The Republic*, was authoritative within reception theory over a long period time. Art, understood as *mimesis*, a term that means both representation and imitation, was believed to trigger in the "receiver" an identification that could be set at a distance only by those who were sufficiently educated and could master their affects. With the advent of print, the fear of the harmful effects of "bad readings" was theorized in particular by the Catholic Church, which equated them at times to poison, at others to venom. Beginning in the eighteenth century, the notion of "moral contagion" (developed by doctors in order to better understand moral panics), collective hysteria, and political uprising (Goldstein 1984) seemed perfectly appropriate for describing the social effects of writings that spread with the rise of print. Shared by revolutionaries and counterrevolutionaries alike, this idealistic belief in the power of words would be reinforced by representations of the role of philosophical works in sparking the French Revolution. Further brandished throughout the nineteenth century against the freedom of the press (Sapiro 2011), this belief established a protosociological precursor to reception theory, relying heavily upon the hierarchy between two reading publics: the educated public, capable of implementing mechanisms of detachment, and the public of new readers, which continued to expand with growing literacy rates and the spread of print (see chapter IV). According to this model, the most vulnerable social categories were women, youth, and the working class; "bad books" supposedly had the power not only to turn them from the straight and narrow, but also to incite them to upset the social order by awakening their aspirations to upward mobility. The tragic characters Julien Sorel in Stendhal's *Le Rouge et le noir* (*The Red and The Black*) and Lucien de Rubempré in Balzac's *Les Illusions perdues* (*Lost Illusions*) gave fuel to this representation of the *déclassés par le haut* (now called "class defectors," following Bourdieu), as being passionate about literature and consumed by social ambition—a portrayal that Barrès would revisit by the end of the nineteenth century in *Les Déracinés* (*The Uprooted*), placing the blame on French republican education, which had been extended to all social classes. The effects of reading were also included in the causal chain of medical pathologies, notably in the case of female hysteria. In *Madame Bovary*, Flaubert combined sociological analysis with medical analysis: Emma Bovary embodied the figure of the new female reader from the *petite bourgeoisie* for whom reading romance novels elicited a desperate desire to escape the confinements of her condition. The cause of her nervous breakdowns, this desire ultimately led her to adultery, bankruptcy, and suicide.

The nascent field of criminology, which sought to catalog the "environmental" effects that could stimulate hereditary defects, gave pride of place to reading. The paradigm of "degeneration" spurred the tracing of literature's harmful effects back to the psychology of writers themselves—an idea developed by Cesare Lombroso, figurehead of the Italian school of positivist criminology, who saw in a fondness for slang and the language of thieves and pimps proof of the degeneracy of the "born criminal." Naturalist writers were thus supposedly suffering from a pathology whose symptoms were obscenity, vulgar language, and amorality. This schema of pseudoscientific analysis was taken up, among other disciplines, by the sociology of art, still embryonic at the time. In *L'Art au point de vue sociologique* (*Art from a Sociological Standpoint*), Jean-Marie Guyau wrote that Zola seemed to have "a natural predisposition to indulge in certain subjects, a predisposition which, according to his very own theories, must be explained by some hereditary cause, some morbid trace" (Guyau 1887, 158).

The Laws of Literary History

The experience of the French Revolution brought about the development of historical analyses comparing countries and national traditions. Germaine de Staël adopted this national framework as a unit for comparison in *De la littérature considérée dans ses rapports avec les institutions sociales* (*Literature Considered in Its Relation to Social Institutions,* originally published in 1800), wherein she set out to define the laws that govern literary history (Staël 1991/2000). Literary genre formed the second unit of comparison specific to this history. The two units were connected by an examination of the sociopolitical conditions that encourage the development of certain genres over others: thus, poetry flourishes under despotism, because its heightened formalism renders it less dangerous. Aside from political structures, de Staël also took into consideration religion and the status of women. While she defended women's writing against those who intended to confine women to the role of literary salon socialites, she was, nevertheless, not above the gendered representations of the division of intellectual labor that prevailed during her time: sentimental literature belonged to women; the literature of ideas belonged to men.

De Staël's analysis was part of a broader reflection on the role of the writer in a liberal[1] society that was meant to be prescriptive: the writer is tasked with embodying perfectibility, the "soul" of the nation, and sensibility. In this respect, the liberal conception of the writer contrasted with that of reactionaries who wanted to keep writers outside politics. Driven by their conviction that men of letters were directly responsible for the Revolution, counterrevolutionary thinkers, and Louis de Bonald in particular, assigned writers a didactic mission of both propagandizing "true" values and prescribing good taste (Bénichou 1996, 117–19). In *L'Ancien Régime et la Révolution* (*The Old Regime and the Revolution*), published in 1856, Alexis de Tocqueville asks himself, "How did men of letters, who possessed neither rank, nor honors, nor wealth, nor responsibility, nor power, become, in fact, the chief statesmen of the time, and even the only ones, since although others ran the government, they alone had authority?" (Tocqueville 2008, 196/1967, 231). According to Tocqueville, this is due to the credibility accorded them in a nation that was "the most literary of all the nations of the world" (2008, 195; 1967, 238). Replacing the old aristocracy, writers had, according to him, constituted an aristocracy of the mind, which after seizing "the direction of opinion" became "a political power in France, and ended up being the most important one" (2008, 198, 200; 1967, 234). This concern about the social role of writers and literature comes up again and again throughout the nineteenth century just as much among the reactionary thinkers as among the republicans[2] and the utopian socialists, from Saint-Simon to Marx. It is most pronounced in France because of the position literature held and because of the authority from which writers benefited, unparalleled in England or in Germany.

It was because of the relationship in France between literature and politics that de Staël employed the notion of "literature" in the broad sense that prevailed in eighteenth-century France and England (Williams 1983), which included philosophy, science, erudition, and *belles lettres*. In 1740 the *Dictionnaire (Dictionary)* of the Académie Française recorded a use of the word restricted to *belles lettres*. This meaning, closer to the contemporary definition of literature, gained a foothold in the beginning of the nineteenth century with the new division of intellectual labor introduced by the professional development of the sciences and the reorganization of academic careers following the Napoleonic educational reforms. The same lexical evolution took place in England (Eagleton 1994, 18).

It was, however, at the margins of the university that research on the laws of literary history was carried out. In the introduction to his *Histoire de la littérature anglaise (History of English Literature)*, published in 1864 and translated into English in 1872, Hippolyte Taine explained that a literary work "is not a mere play of the imagination, the isolated caprice of an excited brain, but a transcript of contemporary manners and customs and the sign of a particular state of intellect" (Taine 1885, 1/1871, t. 1, iii). This presupposition led him to consider literary works as a source of the highest importance for history itself. An avid reader of positivist and scientific ideas, Taine identified three factors that determine the moral state of a civilization and therefore of literary works: "race," which designated "innate dispositions," or "temperament," variable according to the people;[3] "milieu," or environment, namely, the weather and geographic conditions as well as the social and political conditions that shaped the people over time; and the "moment," which referred to the phases of the history of humanity. This method attracted scathing criticism from defenders of a spiritualist conception of creative genius, who condemned its ascription of historical and social causes to literary works as a form of reductionism. Ferdinand Brunetière developed a naturalist conception of the evolution of genres in *L'Évolution des genres dans l'histoire de la littérature* (*The Evolution of Genres in the History of Literature* [1890]): genres are born, they develop, and then they die, depending on whether writers obey or differentiate themselves from them.

These pseudoscientific approaches were soon superseded by literary history, which Gustave Lanson established as a discipline in its own right within the Nouvelle Sorbonne—a development born out of the 1896 republican reforms in higher education. Based on philological methods he imported in part from Germany, Lanson's literary criticism proposed historicizing the social conditions of literary creation. In a lecture on the links between "Literary History and Sociology" presented in 1904 at the École des Hautes Études Sociales at Émile Durkheim's request, Lanson argued that the "'literary phenomenon' was in essence a social phenomenon" (Lanson 1995, 228/1904, 629). Without denying the individual aspect of creation, he explained that the critic's task was to situate the work within the conditions of its production, by taking into account not only the author but also the society of its time, as well as the manner in which it was initially received. He partially replaced the primacy of the individual with "the idea of the individual's relations to various groups and collective entities, the idea of the individual's participation in collective tastes, customs, and states of consciousness" (228/630). It was thus a social history of literature that Lanson called for, transforming the writer into "a social product and social expression" (229/629). There is, in fact, no simple causal link in either direction between the work and the society in which it is produced, but a complex relationship born out of a "communication between an individual and a public" (226/626). Indeed, according to Lanson, readers are not only the recipients of the work, the work also includes them: "The public presides over the works presented to it, but it does so unknowingly" (226/626). This public can be an ideal, imagined one. Moreover, the book is itself "a social phenomenon that evolves": its "effective meaning" is determined neither by the author nor by the methodical critic, but by the public that reads it (229/631). Lanson thus reversed the causality presupposed by "influence studies," developing a veritable precursor to reception theory centered on the forms taken by the successive appropriation of works, albeit without suggesting an adequate methodology of his own. At the end of his article, he articulated a certain number of literary historical laws (see Box 1).

From Worldview to the Sociology of Literary Taste

This research program, which would seem to anticipate the sociology of literature, did not bear fruit apart from Lucien Febvre's masterful study *Le Problème de l'incroyance au XVIe siècle. La Religion de Rabelais* (*The Problem of Unbelief in the Sixteenth Century: The Religion of Rabelais*) (Febvre 2014/1985). First published in 1942, the book anchored literary history within the history of mentalities, following the perspectives opened up by the Annales School against positivist history.[4] It was in Germany that a series of sociological studies of art and literature were published, which attempted to give a social foundation to the idealist notions of *Weltanschauung* (worldview) and *Zeitgeist* (spirit of the age) by relating them to particular social groups. Inspired by Max Weber and Werner Sombart, Alfred von Martin devoted himself to the study of the Florentine haute bourgeoisie in his

Box 1. The Laws of Literary History according to Gustave Lanson

Lanson states six laws of literary history:

- The "Law of correlation between literature and life": "Literature is the expression of society." Literature depends on social institutions (such as political regimes) without, however, being reduced to them; it can also describe atypical realities, or alter their features to aesthetic ends, or even express protest against prevailing mores or the social condition.

- The "Law of foreign influences": Small nations tend to borrow artistic and literary models from larger ones. But the borrowings happen by way of appropriation and adaptation, and fill various social functions. For example, "the Germans' use of England to resist French influence" (Lanson 1995, 232).

- The "Law of the crystallization of genres": This operates according to three conditions: the existence of masterpieces, a technique allowing for imitation, and a doctrine that orders it. Once crystallized, genres have, like social facts, a constraining character on future generations.

- The "Law of correlation between forms and aesthetic aims": If forms are at times created for aesthetic purposes, Lanson asserts having frequently observed an inverse temporal correlation between the phases of genre crystallization and the aesthetic benefits that follow the experimental stages.

Sociology of the Renaissance in 1932. The previous year Levin L. Schücking's *The Sociology of Literary Taste* was published.

If the materialist approach promoted by Schücking intended to break with the idealism of the "spirit of the age," it also positioned itself against Brunetière's scientific naturalism. Following William Dilthey's distinction between the methods of the

- The fifth law describes the conditions of the appearance of masterpieces: they must be understood as the result of a series of cultural productions that prepare their advent as much as their acceptance by educating the public and creating expectations, without which the work would scandalize.

- The last law concerns the way books act upon their publics: if the public is present in a book from the start, the book exerts, in turn, an effect on its readers. "The book is not only a sign, but also a contributor to the public spirit," explains Lanson. It helps to shape and direct the collective consciousness of an era. "The power of the writer operates as a succession of crystallizations of public opinion." Voltaire, for instance, provided eighteenth-century French society with the watchwords "tolerance" and "humanity." Dickens mobilized the sensibility of his contemporaries toward the reform of schools and prisons.

Against the causal conception of the influence of books, Lanson nevertheless reminds us once more that the book is "less a creative force than an organizing force." He equates the writer with the conductor who plays the role of coordination. This is what makes literature a significant authority, especially in a democratic state (Lanson 1995, 230–34).

sciences of the mind (*Geisteswissenschaften*) and those of the natural sciences, Schücking proposed replacing the vitalistic explanation of the evolution of literary genres with a strictly sociological explanation that takes into account both the position of the artist in society and the characteristics of his or her audience. Thus, the patronage model had a determining effect on artistic production prior to the advent of a market, which allowed artists and authors to live off their work. While the aristocracy granted a purely decorative role to the arts, the educated middle class (*Bildungsbürgertum*) accorded them a higher function, making creators into prophets of human conscience and the embodiment of freedom. Their rise to grandeur as nineteenth-century literary heroes testifies to this change of status, as does the fact that the nobility could devote themselves openly to the arts from then on. The "art for art's sake" movement, which shielded creators from ordinary morality, was the most extreme manifestation of this new cult. It also aimed to free them from the public's *diktat*; the circle of recognition limited itself to a "mutual admiration society" composed of peers and critics (Schücking 1966, 25). This configuration is characteristic of the formation of groups bearing a new aesthetic into circles—or what we would today call a network of relations. This is the precondition for artistic innovation, since one cannot create in isolation and it is difficult to champion new aesthetic forms in the face of the dominant taste. This literary circle, however, was not sufficient; Schücking insisted upon the importance of consecrating authorities, "guards of the entrance to the temple of literary fame" (42), such as publishers and theater directors; while the majority of them, driven by financial considerations, prefer to stick to safe investments, some do support novelty. Publishers became important in the eighteenth century, when patrons disappeared. Schücking called for the development of a history of publishing to shed light on the evolution of literary taste, including the materialist study of books themselves (for example, the norm of publishing books in three volumes, called "triple-deckers," that prevailed in the nineteenth century to such an extent that one-volume novels risked rejection). Among the authorities that take part in the selection process, Schücking also highlighted the role of critics, even though, according to a study done by the association of the

German book trade (Börsenverein des Deutschen Buchhandels) in Leipzig in 1926, only 160 books had been bought solely on the basis of a critic's opinion, versus 390 acquired following an acquaintance's recommendation. Societies for the promotion of individual authors (for instance, the Samuel Beckett Society), cultural associations, public libraries, and lending libraries have also participated in the circulation of literature since the eighteenth century. Finally, schools and universities continue to preserve and perpetuate standards of taste.

In addition to the historical relativism implied by the theories of worldview and of taste, these studies introduced a kind of social relativity, varying by group, by questioning some groups' ability to impose their worldviews and tastes on others. Interrupted by the rise of the Nazi regime, these studies circulated again after the war in English translation with support from Karl Mannheim, who published them in his Routledge sociology series.

Whereas the problematics regarding "worldviews" were reworked within Marxist-inspired thought, reflections on the conditions of production and the circulation of texts developed in France, in the wake of the Sartrean conception of literature as an act of communication. English cultural studies attempted to articulate the two questions together.

Literature as an Act of Communication

In 1958 the first *Que sais-je* book on the "sociology of literature" was published (Escarpit 1958/1971). In 1960, its author, Robert Escarpit, established Le Centre de Sociologie des Faits Littéraires (Center for the Sociology of Literary Facts) at the University of Bordeaux; the center later became the Institut de Littérature et de Techniques Artistiques de Masse (Institute of Literature and Mass Artistic Techniques; ILTAM). Following

Sartre (see Box 2), Escarpit considered literature to be an act of communication.

The reflection on the evolution of modes of communication coincided with the interests of media studies, which was then burgeoning, and from which Escarpit borrowed certain orientations for the sociology of literature. As an act of communication, literature involves three parties: the producer, the distributor, and the consumer. A research program was associated with each: the social conditions of production, surveys on book production and the means of dissemination, and studies on reading. Recourse to quantitative methods allowed researchers to meet the demands of publishers and public authorities who, amid an expanding market and a growing interest in the conditions that favor the democratization of culture, were keen to have data. This program led to a sociology of publishing and a sociology of reading, two fields that developed separately thereafter (see chapters II and IV). Studying producers entails analyzing the distribution of literary generations by period, the social and geographic origins of writers and their profession, the funding of literary activity, and the conditions governing the work of writing (copyright laws, status, and types of compensation).

This positivist approach, however, remains insufficiently problematized, sociologically speaking—from its sampling methods to its reflection on socioprofessional categories and its general analysis. Furthermore, this approach does not allow us to grasp the specificity of literature as a social activity. It is typical of external analysis, which tends to reduce works to their material conditions of production and reception, with little regard for the logics unique to the universe of symbolic production and the production of literary value.

Box 2. Literature as an Act of Communication

Sartre develops the idea that literature is an act of communication in *What Is Literature* (1948). He defines reading, along with writing, as an act. The book, he explains, "is not, like the tool, a means for any end whatever; the end to which it offers itself is the reader's freedom" (1988a, 47/1993a, 54). This is why Sartre rejects the Kantian definition of the work of art as "purposive without purpose." If he agrees with Kant that a work of art has no end, it is only because it is in and of itself an end. For it exists only if one looks at it. And reading is not a simple game but a commitment by the reader, who appeals to their freedom and their own creative power to make the work exist. Reading appears thus to be a "pact of generosity between author and reader" (62). The author obliges the reader to "create" what they "reveal," therefore to compromise themselves. With this act, the author reflects back to the reader their own freedom and responsibility.

The communicative function that Sartre ascribes to literature enabled him to define the mission of the writer in the contemporary period. This mission evolved over time. Once the spiritual was divorced from the temporal* and the clerics formed a separate profession, who wrote for the narrow audience of their peers, the writer could in good conscience withdraw into themselves. But the growth of readership as a result of literacy attached a new, universal mission to the writer that the development of the press and radio reinforced. From that point on, the writer could no longer limit themselves to an audience of specialists. This mission came into focus for Sartre during the German occupation of France in World War II. The freedom to write implies, of course, a citizen's freedom. The art of prose cannot accommodate any political regime; it must stand with democracy, the only system in which writing still holds meaning. If the writer's responsibility results from their creative freedom, they have the responsibility to guarantee freedom in return.

Here, "temporal" means "mundane," referring to Auguste Comte's distinction between spiritual and temporal power.

Moving beyond Reflection Theory:
Genetic Structuralism vs. Cultural Studies

At a time when literary theory (New Criticism and Structuralism) was withdrawing into an internal analysis of texts, the sociology of literature was developing within Marxist thought. According to the materialist premise, literature, like religion, participates in the superstructure, which reflects the relations of production. While it appeared from the outset reductionist, reflection theory nevertheless gave rise to rich discussions about the autonomy of works in relation to social conditions and the mediations between them (Goldmann 1970/1968; Macherey 1971/1978; Williams 1977). Is literature a simple reflection of society, as literary realism claimed, or is it the expression of an ideology that conveys a worldview? Is this worldview the manifestation of the collective consciousness of the ruling class, or does it echo the contradictions that shape the social relations of production? These were the types of questions taken up by Marxist theorists (see Sayre 2011).

Unlike the biographical approach that held sway in the scholarly tradition, the ultimate example of which is Sartre's 1971–72 book on Flaubert (a study incorporating the contributions of Marxism and psychoanalysis), the Marxist approach consisted in shifting the analysis from the level of the individual to that of the collective. From the point of view of its objects and its methods, the Marxist-inspired sociology of literature took two distinct tracks. One, centered on the analysis of literary works, following Hungarian critic György Lukács (author of *Soul and Form* [1974], *The Theory of the Novel* [1971], *The Historical Novel* [1962], and *Studies in European Realism* [1950]), examined the relationship between literary forms and the social situations out of which they emerged, a relationship mediated by the collective consciousness. The other, which was developed by the founders of cultural studies, first appeared in Antonio Gramsci's *Prison Notebooks* and took further shape in Arnold Hauser's *The Social History of Art*, focused on the social conditions of the production and reception of artistic works.

Using the work of Lukács, the Franco-Romanian critic Lucien Goldmann developed Genetic Structuralism (Goldmann 1964/1975). For Goldmann, the real subject of the work is not the individual author but the social group to which the author belongs. The group's worldview constitutes the mediation between social and economic infrastructure and literary works. There is a structural homology between Racine's tragedies or Pascal's *Pensées* and the Jansenist worldview, which is an expression of the collective consciousness of the nobility of the robe (Goldmann 1955/2016). Theorists from the Frankfurt School also addressed the problematics of reflection. In his *Notes to Literature* (1958), Theodor W. Adorno observed that the most hermetic art can express a reaction against language "sullied by commerce" (Adorno 1991). But by insisting on the ambiguity of literary texts, their polysemy, he also showed that they resist being reduced to ideology.

At the same time, the major works of cultural studies appeared in England: *The Uses of Literacy* (1957) by Richard Hoggart, *Culture and Society* (1958) and *The Long Revolution* (1961) by Raymond Williams. Whereas the Frankfurt School had condemned mass culture as a mystification alienating the consciousness of the working class, Hoggart turned it into an object of study in its own right for the sociology of literature, and laid the foundations of a sociology of the reception of works through his study of working-class reading habits. Criticizing the theory, shared by traditionalists and Marxists alike, which posited that the working classes were nothing more than passive receptacles of cultural industries, Hoggart introduced the concept of "oblique" reading, which characterized the detachment of readers from disadvantaged classes (Hoggart 2009, 213). In

an article where he posed the problem of the conditions for de-
mocratizing access to "high culture," Raymond Williams (1974)
distinguished popular literature produced "by" the people (folk),
from modern mass literature, produced "for" the people. Having
studied the emergence of the notion of culture in the Romantic
period and the effects of the Industrial Revolution on literature
(Williams 1983, 1965), Williams implemented a research program for the historical sociology of institutions of literary life
(publishers, journals, learned societies, circles), which resulted
more broadly in the sociology of culture and communication
(Williams 1977, 1981). While for Goldmann it is the worldview
that constitutes a mediation between the economic and social
infrastructure and the work, for Williams, it is the social conditions of production of works.

"Production" is the concept with which Pierre Macherey,
a Marxist literary theorist close to Althusser, proposed to replace "creation." A work of literature is indeed "the product of
a labour" and the writer "a workman" who "does not manufac-
ture the materials with which he works" (Macherey 1978, 137, 41;
1971, 53–54). This concept is in contradiction with the Romantic
idea of production, theorized by Sartre in *What Is Literature?*
and according to which the writer, in producing their own "rules
of production," "measures," and "criteria," differentiates themself from the artisan whose work is the product of impersonal
traditional norms—which makes the writer the ultimate embodiment of freedom (Sartre 1988b, 49/1975, 47). However, like
Althusser, Macherey also rejected a purely materialist approach
of the conditions of production.

In *Reading Capital*, Louis Althusser (1965/1970) and his disciples critiqued two types of causality in history: mechanical
causality (Cartesian), which supposes an extrinsic cause; and
expressive causality, which considers the elements of a structure
as expressions of a totality (theorized by Leibniz, it underpins

all of Hegelian philosophy), and which they reproached for its essentialist premise. This two-pronged critique also took aim at Marxist analyses: both reflection theory and explanations in terms of worldview, which understand texts as allegorical models of society as a whole (as is the case in Lukács's work, for example). The concept of mediation, which Althusser likened to expressive causality, poses a problem in that it establishes relations between different levels (superstructure and infrastructure, text and society). Althusser proposed to replace these two types of causality with what he called "structural causality," a term that refers to the presence of the structure—its immanence—in its effects, much like the concept of *Darstellung* in the Marxist theory of value.

Discussing these objections in *The Political Unconscious*, the American Marxist critic Frederic Jameson (1981) defended the local validity of the first two types of causality: according to him, it is hardly debatable that the replacement of the dominant model of publishing the novel in three volumes with the format of a single, less expensive volume after the crisis within the publishing industry at the end of the nineteenth century (external cause) brought about a change in the form of narrative fiction; likewise, if expressive or allegorical causality operates at a certain level, it is because grand narratives or the prevailing conceptions of history are often inscribed in the texts themselves. These are even, according to Jameson, our main intermediary toward an otherwise inaccessible historicity, which functions as an absent cause as defined by Spinoza. It is in this way that they constitute sources for understanding our "political unconscious," which must be the purpose of the work of interpretation.

For Jameson, Althusser's major contribution resides in the relative autonomy that he recognized in different social spheres, unlike the expressive causality that tends to reduce them using concepts such as structural homology (for example, in Goldmann's work, between the class position, worldview, and artistic forms, or between the novel as form and daily life in the individualistic society born out of the market economy) and mediation (the institution of the family as mediation between the child's experience and class structure, for example, in Sartre's biography of Flaubert). But, as Jameson emphasized, the notion of relative autonomy cannot be conceived without a reflection on the forms of mediation between different spheres.

Functionalism, Interactionism, and the Relational Approach

While Marxist and positivist approaches were interested in the conditions of production of literary works, they did not treat the literary world as a specific universe possessing its own logics. By constrast, various theories developed in the 1970s approached the literary world as a field, as an institution, or as a system, interpreting this universe as the primary mediation between literary works and their conditions of production. Jacques Dubois's institutional approach and Itamar Even-Zohar's polysystem theory (1990) therefore addressed the concerns that also gave birth to Pierre Bourdieu's field theory, which made literature a full-fledged object of study for sociology (Bourdieu 1983, 1996). Despite their shared object, these theories differ as much theoretically as methodologically. Structural or relational approaches (field theory) will be distinguished here from both functionalist approaches (polysystem theory and the theory of literary institutions) and interactionist approaches (Howard Becker's "art worlds"). Partially incompatible in their principles, they underscore different aspects of the literary world.

Field Theory

Field theory works under the assumption that literature is not a socially undetermined activity. Nevertheless, literature cannot be reduced to social, economic, or political determinants. It is an activity with its own laws, specific stakes, and principles of consecration, which are relatively autonomous from external constraints. Originally Marxist, the notion of autonomy, which offered a corrective to reflection theory, was entirely redefined by Pierre Bourdieu, leading to the elaboration of the concept of -field (Bourdieu 1983, 1984a/1993a, 1986, 1992/1996, 1993b, 2017, 2022).[5]

The concept of field refers to the "space of possibles" available to writers in the form of choices to be made between options more or less established as such over the course of the field's history (for instance, rhyme or free verse; an extradiegetic or an intradiegetic narrator; an indirect, direct, or free indirect style). A field presupposes a belief, or *illusio*, that drives its participants to comply with the rules of the game in effect in this space. Aesthetic choices correlate with the positions that writers occupy in the field. These positions are defined depending on the volume and the configuration of specific symbolic capital held, which is to say, on the degree and type of recognition that they benefit from as writers, symbolic recognition (by peers or critics) not necessarily implying temporal success (sales, institutional consecration), and vice versa. There is therefore a structural homology between the space of positions and the space of position takings.

The structure of the space of positions is thus determined by the unequal distribution of specific capital. The structure primarily opposes well-known writers, who hold a dominant position and can as a result impose their conception of literature, and those who hold a dominated position, generally the newcomers or marginalized writers. This division between "dominant" and "dominated" writers (for example, the members of the Académie Française vs. literary bohemians) comes from a more general sociological principle of opposition between the "established" and the "outsiders," or between "veterans" and "newcomers"; but in the literary field, it takes on very distinctive forms, linked to modes of accumulating symbolic capital specific to this universe. Indeed, since Romanticism, which propounded the law of originality, the avant-garde (for example, the Surrealists) has asserted itself by contesting the dominant conceptions of literature of its time.

Another opposition structuring the literary field is the tension between forces of autonomy and forces of heteronomy, which those who defend the autonomy of aesthetic judgment in relation to extraliterary, ethical-political and economic constraints have to resist. The forms these principles of opposition take vary depending on sociohistorical configurations. For example, autonomy was embodied at times by "art for art's sake," and at others by political commitment (Jurt 1992; Sapiro 2014).

A field of forces, the literary world is also a battlefield. The dynamic of change stems from the confrontations between dominants, whose best interest is in maintaining the existing power relations, and the dominated, who struggle to overthrow those relations. In situations of relative autonomy, the confrontation operates according to the specific rules of the field: mastery of the principles of versification, theatrical composition, and novel writing, without which aspiring writers will find themselves excluded from the game. Autonomy is characterized by the principle of "autotelism," the idea that a work is an end in itself, and by the principle of self-referentiality, namely, the act of making reference to the history of the field, which requires specific expertise from social agents, reflecting in turn their inherited dispositions (from their family) and acquired dispositions (in the framework of their intellectual training)—that is, their habitus, to use another of Bourdieu's concepts. In contrast, situations of considerable heteronomy are characterized by the intervention of extraliterary forces to mediate internal conflicts in the field, according to ethical, political, and economic criteria, to which aesthetic issues are subordinated (see, for example, Sapiro 2014).

The methodological autonomization of the literary field as a sociological object of study is therefore possible, provided, however, that we understand the sociohistorical factors of its autonomization from political, economic, and religious constraints (Bourdieu 1985b). In *The Rules of Art*, Bourdieu (1996) studies the emergence of a pole of small-scale production that pits aesthetic judgment expressed by peers against the economic criteria of success (sales figures) that prevail at the pole of large-scale production of publishing (see chapter II). Furthermore, this autonomy is always relative: the external constraints never stop weighing on literary activity, but they never do so directly—they are *refracted* (or retranslated) depending on the field's internal stakes, rules of operation, and principles of structuration.[6]

The Literary Institution

Systematizing an idea first used by Harry Levin (1946) and then by Marxist thinkers such as Renée Balibar, Jacques Dubois, a professor of French literature at the University of Liège, defined the literary institution as an ensemble of social facts that contribute to instituting literary practices, including writing, and moreover, as an "ensemble of norms applicable to a particular activity and defining a legitimacy that is expressed in a charter or a code" (Dubois 2005, 31, our translation). In keeping with Bourdieu's principle of the relative autonomy of the literary field, Dubois attempts to connect this with the Althusserian concept of the "ideological state apparatus" in order to explore the relationship between literature and ideology. His approach also integrates methods from sociocriticism, developed by Claude Duchet (1979), in accordance with Marxist thought. Through the study of the inscription of the "social" within texts, Dubois aims to detect the ideological dimension of literary works and the representations of the social world that they convey. Likewise, his approach incorporates the study of literature as "social discourse," following the research program mapped out by Canadian literary scholar Marc Angenot (see chapter III).

The literary institution encompasses the two spheres of production (small- and large-scale), the social functions of literature, the institutions of production, the legitimizing authorities, reading conditions, the status of the writer, and that of the text and the national literature and genres to which it belongs. Under the umbrella of "minority" literatures, Dubois includes banned, popular, parallel, primitive, and regional literatures, which he defines in relation to their subordination to dominant culture. This terminology, like Deleuze and Guattari's "minor literatures," echoes the notion of "small literatures," developed by Kafka. Among them, Dubois mentions the case of national literatures with weak autonomy, such as Belgian, Swiss, and Québécois literatures, which are dependent upon Paris. An entire domain of research has opened up on this subject (Bourdieu 1985a; Gauvin and Bertrand 2003; Aron 2005; Leperlier 2022).

It should be noted, however, that the term "minor" has less descriptive power regarding the status of these literatures than does the notion of their "dominated" position in relation to the dominant culture, or their "peripheral" situation in relation to a "center." The concepts of center and periphery are well adapted to the representation of spatial relations; this is how they have been used by Latin American dependency theory and by Immanuel Wallerstein in his world system theory. Polysystem theory uses them in a more general and systematic way, to describe the relationships between different types of literary productions.

Polysystem Theory

Developed in the 1970s, polysystem theory experienced various reformulations up until 1990 (Even-Zohar 1990). Building on the theories of the Russian formalists and the Prague linguistic circle (Todorov 2001), Itamar Even-Zohar, professor of literary theory at the University of Tel Aviv, drew upon the latter's dynamic functionalism, which was lacking in French structuralism, and which allowed for the development of a historical approach to literature. Breaking with an essentialist conception of literary works, the notion of the "system" connects the different elements that constitute it by examining the functions they fulfill, thereby avoiding a disaggregating, historicist positivism. That notion of the "polysystem" takes into account the heterogeneity of the observed phenomena and the coexistence of different stratified systems.

Even-Zohar defines the system of literature as comprising the activities designated as literary and the network of relations that produces them. To reconstruct the network, he adapts Jakobson's model of communication (see Figure 1): the literary system refers to the relations between producers (writers) and consumers (readers), which are mediated on one hand by the "institution" (publishers, journals, critics, groups of writers, state authorities, the educational system, the media, and so on) and the "repertoire," and on the other hand by the "market," which includes not only points of distribution and sale, such as bookstores and libraries, but also all the actors and activities involved in the circulation of the "product," overlapping partly with the "institution" in this way.

The dynamic of change depends on the evolution of the relations between the center and the periphery— for example, when an element is transferred from a peripheral system (popular literature, minority literature, literature in translation) to a central

FIGURE 1. The Literary System

INSTITUTION [Context]

Repertoire [Code]

PRODUCER [addresser] _____ CONSUMER [addressee]

("writer") ("reader")

MARKET [contact/channel]

Product [message]

Source: Even-Zohar (1990, 31)

system—as well as on transformations of the principles of hierarchization, effected through the *canonization process*. Theorized by Viktor Shklovsky at the beginning of the 1920s, the canonization process, by legitimizing certain literary devices, genres, and authors, shifts them to the center of the system, at the expense of other elements relegated to the periphery (this mechanism is responsible for the disqualification of epigones).

The concept of "repertoire," coined by Even-Zohar, designates all the laws and models (themes, styles, linguistic options) that govern the production of texts. It distinguishes the "available" items of a system's repertoire, which are frequently mobilized, from "accessible" items, which may be seldom used at a given point in time, but are nevertheless present in the shared "stock" of options; it also tracks the circulation of both through borrowings and transpositions. The concept also distinguishes between the canonicity of models and the canonicity of texts: the fact that a text enters a culture's canon is not enough to turn it into a model to be followed. It is the canonicity of models that is decisive for the system's dynamic. Finally, the concept distinguishes conservative repertoires, reluctant to accept the introduction of new items, and therefore more predictable, from innovative repertoires, open to outside models, and therefore less predictable. The phases of construction of national literatures and situations of cultural dependence (as was the case with Hebrew-language literature with respect to Russian literature at the beginning of the twentieth century) were thus characterized by a massive importation of foreign models.

The "transfers" of repertoire items (or "repertoremes") take place not only within a polysystem but between polysystems, which are themselves stratified, forming a "mega-polysystem." While during the Middle Ages and the Renaissance, the republic of letters in Europe formed a polysystem in which the center was represented by writings in Latin and the periphery was represented by texts in vernacular languages, the creation of national identities eroded this polysystem. Nevertheless, the transfers between national literatures were still governed by hierarchical relations between center and periphery: French literature held the central position, followed by German literature. As a founder of translation studies, which was further developed by his student Gideon Toury and by José Lambert's team at the Leuven Language Institute, Even-Zohar was one of the first to call attention to the role that translation played in the crystallization of national cultures, a phenomenon largely left out of literary history until very recently. One of the main contributions of polysystem theory was to move the focus from the culture of origin (source culture) to the culture of reception (target culture), by thinking about the mechanisms of text selection and about translation norms.

Field, Literary Institution, and Polysystem: A Theoretical and Methodological Comparison

Breaking with an essentialist conception of literary works, the concepts of field, literary institution, and (poly)system propose situating works within their social conditions of production. Nevertheless, far from reducing literary works to their external conditions, these three approaches understand literature in its specificity, by placing it within a system of relatively autonomous relations (the space of possibles, the institution, the repertoire of models), structured according to its own principles of stratification and hierarchization.

This system of relations is dynamic, not static: it is a question of studying the transformation of the principles of hierarchization (like the legitimization of the detective novel, or of jazz music) and the mechanisms of consecration and canonization of literary works. The functionalist concept of system, however, risks presupposing an equilibrium within a given system, whereas the notion of field examines the state of the relations between the forces present in the field.[7] This is a risk that polysystem theory escapes by its assumption of a plurality of coexisting systems, by its historical dimension, and by its dynamic approach. Nevertheless, being centered on texts that serve as a basis for the reconstruction of the repertoire of available models, "polysystem" theory is limited to seeking an explanation for cultural transformations in the self-regulating dynamics of the system, in the absence of any sociological analysis of cultural producers and their audiences. By contrast, field theory focuses first on the social agents of the literary field, both individuals and institutions. Also developed by literary scholars who prioritize textual analysis, the theory of the literary institution, for its part, interrogates the mediations between "the literary" and "the social" (inferred from the texts themselves) as if they were two distinct entities, while field theory explores the mediations between the social conditions of production and literary works.

Structural, institutional, and systemic approaches also enable us to systematize the comparison between cultures and between time periods by defining the comparable elements and by bringing out meaningful differences, whether those are the conditions of production, the space of possibles, the repertoire, the principles of hierarchization (canonical vs. noncanonical lit-

erature), or social trajectories. Therefore, one can only understand the singularity of a work and the innovativeness of its style
at a given time by reconstructing the space of possibles in which
it was produced, or the repertoire available to its author (for example, in the case of Flaubert's groundbreaking use of free indirect discourse in *Madame Bovary,* borrowed from Goethe). For
this purpose, one needs to systematically compare the narrative
forms deployed in a given era, after having traced the contours
of the relevant corpus.

The conditions of production must also be subjected to a
rigorous comparative analysis, cutting across both time periods and cultures. It is necessary, however, to have a minimum
of comparable data, starting with the existence of a relatively
autonomized social activity designated by the term "literature."
Only with the use of European languages, a result of colonialism,
did the question of African literature(s), in the modern meaning
of a written literature, emerge in the twentieth century, despite
a longstanding oral tradition on the continent. A comparative
approach thus helps to relativize this notion of "literature" and
examine its social status during different periods and in different cultures.

For each context, the (poly)systemic approach empirically
studies the elements that enter into relation with each other
within the framework of literary activity, without normatively
determining what is or is not literature in advance. Moving
beyond the canon of consecrated works, the polysystemic approach expands to include noncanonical texts, what were once
called "paraliterature," which is to say, minor or popular genres
or subgenres (detective or romance novels, for instance), or youth
literature. The opposition between "canonical" and "noncanonical" allows for the comparison of literary systems according to
the hierarchy of legitimacy. Likewise, the concept of a repertoire
of available or accessible models also allows for a comparison

of systems: for example, rhyme, which constituted an absolute poetic constraint until the end of the nineteenth century in European poetry, was abandoned at the beginning of the twentieth century, and has effectively been forbidden since the 1950s; yet poems in classic verse have not been excluded from the canon (they belong to the accessible repertoire, but not to the available one).

Beyond the study of principles of hierarchization and of the space of possibles, field theory, like polysystem theory, opens up possibilities for comparison at different levels. In the first place, the degree of the literary field's autonomy can be estimated through an analysis of its dependency upon the state (control and management of production) and the market (see chapter II). On a second level, one can compare the principles undergirding the field's structure at different historical moments and in different national contexts, depending on the oppositions that obtain between the dominants and the dominated and between the forces of autonomy and heteronomy, which also establish a structural homology between different fields (for instance, the literary field and the political field [Sapiro 2018a]). The comparison of writers' individual or collective trajectories sheds light on the connection between the space of possibles and social characteristics, opening up questions about the links between literature and identity and about the scholastic habitus. However, just as research on French-speaking countries, examining the autonomy of Belgian, Swiss, or Québécois literature in relation to the French literary field (Bourdieu 1985a; Maggetti 1995; Aron 2005), leads us to question the geographic and symbolic borders of fields, so too does the inclusion of colonial and postcolonial perspectives (see chapter III; also Fonkoua and Halen [2001]; Ducournau [2017]).

Symbolic Interactionism

The interactionist approach is often spontaneously taken by biographers and literary historians who are interested in context: relationships within the family, friendships, love interests, group formations, relationships with peers, publishers, translators. This approach is strongly favored by the type of sources that we have for writers, particularly rich for this purpose: correspondence, personal testimonies, memoirs, autobiographical accounts, and so on. And, indeed, the less the activity is institutionalized, the more the relationships within the production chain are personal, and the more interactions determine the particular space. Contrary to the impersonality that governs the bureaucratic world, personal relationships, which are poorly regulated and based on charisma, in the Weberian sense, take precedence in the universes of symbolic production. Sociologically speaking, the world of letters is therefore a privileged space for understanding the system of relations between individuals. It lends itself just as well to the qualitative approaches of symbolic interactionism as to network analysis.

Centered on the "cooperative network" of suppliers, distributors, performers, dealers, and critics, the interactionist approach developed by US sociologist Howard Becker (2008) for studying "art worlds" has the merit of introducing intermediaries—not only the "core producers" who directly contribute to artistic value, such as publishers or translators, but also those whom Becker calls "support personnel," including, for example, in today's publishing world publishers, copyeditors, public relations managers, and sales representatives. These "support personnel" participate in the production of value (through activities of promotion and circulation). Becker thus emphasizes that artistic production is founded upon a more or less stabilized division of labor between different categories of workers who each work on a "bundle of tasks" (a term coined by Everett Hughes), and who impose constraints on the artists (for example, the format of three volumes required in the nineteenth century for English novels, or its limitation to one volume starting at the end of the century). The recruitment of support personnel, regarded as being interchangeable, is a part of the mobilization of human resources necessary for the production of the artwork, alongside the mobilization of material resources. This often requires that artists fund their project themselves (the case of self-publishing, in which authors have their books printed at their own expense, is illustrative for literature), or else find cultural patronage.

Collaborative work relies on "conventions," which save time but also run the risk of becoming rote. These conventions take the form of relatively routinized procedures and more or less established forms (certain genres or subgenres, such as the sonnet or the detective novel, are constraining, while other genres, such as the literary novel, are more flexible), adaptations (in the theater, for example), and receptions.

Even though the interactionist approach is focused on cooperation, it does not overlook conflicts that can arise over the definition of these tasks or over differences between conventions. While, as for functionalism, the equilibrium of social systems producing art depends on the conditions that maintain processes already in effect, the maintenance of these processes in these conditions is not necessary but contingent, according to interactionists: the equilibrium of the system depends on actors who interact and whom functionalism does not take into account. This is not to mention that the division of labor can be unstable and can become an object of negotiation, for example, between a publisher and a printer at the beginning of the nineteenth century, or nowadays between a publisher and a literary agent (Sapiro and Leperlier 2021).

Interactionism opens up a whole field of research covered by the umbrella of the sociology of work within the artistic field, but it has been little explored in the domain of literature beyond a study dedicated to the chain of book production in the United States, conducted by Lewis Coser, Charles Kadushin, and Walter Powell (1982), and more recently the analysis of the process by which a book is produced by Clayton Childress (2019). In France, the sociology of publishing has made more use of field theory than of the interactionist approach (see chapter II).

Cultural intermediaries are not only part of a cooperative network but also play a major role in producing the belief in the value of artworks, that is to say, their symbolic capital, as argued by Bourdieu (1977/1993b, 74–111). Bruno Latour distinguishes intermediaries, who do not affect the meaning of the work they produce and sell, from mediators, who transform its signification. While translators and critics could be taken as examples of the latter, studying the practices of agents of publishers reveals that they often do intervene in the contents of texts—for example, their titles—as well as in their presentation to the public, and thus their meaning. Therefore, it seems more relevant to define cultural intermediaries as those who specialize in marketing cultural products (agents, publishers), and mediators as those who specialize in their interpretation (translators, and critics). Moreover, we should distinguish between the "core" intermediaries (publishers, literary agents), who play a major role in establishing the literary work as such and thus act as gatekeepers to the literary field, and their "support personnel" (copyeditors, proofreaders, sales representatives, public relations staff, rights managers), who help them in this task.

Becker's interactionist approach is limited to external analysis, but there is nothing to prevent it from being extended to the production of the works themselves, to include, for instance, the series of interactions that lead to the publication of a book; feedback from the first readers to whom the author entrusts their

manuscript; and feedback from the professionals (editor, pre-
parer, proofreader) who take part in what the historian Roger
Chartier (1988, 1994, 1996, 2021) calls the *"mise en livre,"* and
who contribute to modifying the text and its meaning, as Donald
Mackenzie (1999) also underscored. Thus, the title is sometimes
suggested by a third party (reviewer or editor); furthermore,
what is called the "packaging" (and which tends to become a
specialized task that can be outsourced)—that is, formatting,
illustrations, front and back cover design, and the publisher's
presentation—all shape the reception of the work (see chapter
IV). These aspects, which attracted the attention of book historians, are also taken into account in the sociology of publishing, translation, and reception. For instance, Clayton Childress
(2019) studies the trajectory of *Jarrettsville*, a historical novel by
Cornelia Nixon published in 2009, through the entire editorial
process, from its initial composition to its reception by reviewers
and readers.

Networks

Network analysis was developed in US sociology in the 1980s as a
way of moving beyond the functionalist paradigm that described
society in terms of classes, groups, roles, statuses, and organizations, as well as the institutional approach, better adapted to
older societies. Networks also enable researchers to connect the
macrosocial level of the structure, on which the functionalists
focus, with the microsocial level of interactions, by measuring
"social capital" and by studying the structure of relationships.
Network analysis first developed within the scope of economic
sociology, and remains influenced by economic thought and its
favorite objects of study (companies).

Just like the "field," "institution," and "polysystem" approaches, network analysis is a means of breaking with the

vision of the singularity of the "creator," which too often results in its methodological isolation, by placing the emphasis back on the collective dimension of the literary activity. However, the paradigm of networks, which circulated in both intellectual and literary history, without ever being truly theorized, seems better able than institutional or systemic approaches to describe the interactions that literary activity gives rise to, the modes of group formation it involves (literary circles, literary schools, journals, avant-garde movements, and so forth), and their modes of mobilization (signing manifestos and petitions, forming associations or ad hoc groups of authors, and so on). Furthermore, beyond cultural resources, social capital plays a very important role in gaining access to literary and publishing milieux, which operate by cooptation. The network approach, however, is not without its own drawbacks and limitations.

Unlike field theory, which emphasizes objective relations, network theory is interested in interactions, conceived as contexts of individual action. Network analysis tends to dissociate social capital from other types of capital in order to measure its relative effects (to show, for example, that social capital takes precedence over cultural capital in the acquisition of a first job), while field theory emphasizes the joint action of different types of resources: a good knowledge of the rules of the game (cultural capital) along with relationships in the literary and publishing milieu (social capital in the field) constitute a pathway into the literary field, their accumulation multiplying one's chances of entering into the game.

This leads us to an even more important difference between the two theories. The relational approach implied in field theory is irreducible to interactions. Modeled on phonology, which is interested in meaningful differences, field theory posits that individuals define themselves in relation to one another independent of actual relationships, which can of course exist or materialize at a given moment, but may also mask objective relations: thus, a strongly competitive relationship between two individuals is often the expression of the proximity of the positions they hold. In the fields of cultural production, position-takings more or less contribute to redefining the space of relevant problematics. It is the distance between these positions that produces the difference that makes each stand out from the other. The fields are battlefields, structured around oppositions and conflicts, often expressed in the social agents' own representations, which orient actions as much as positive references and friendships. The choice of an adversary can be an intentional and conscious strategy to maintain one's position. It is only fitting that, in the wake of the liberation of Paris at the end of World War II, it is said that François Mauriac, while reading an article by his younger peer Albert Camus arguing in favor of a harsh *épuration* (purge), exclaimed, "There's my sparring partner!" (quoted by Lacouture 1980, 189). He thereupon engaged in a months-long written duel with Camus, who was at the time the editor of the newspaper *Combat*. This choice hid another: Mauriac's refusal to engage in dialogue with Sartre, who had eviscerated one of his novels five years before.

One of network theory's major contributions is that it takes into account the conditions of access to information and correlates those with the chances of a certain type of relationship developing between two or more actors. For example, in "cliques," networks in which individuals almost all have close relationships with one another, the relation between the number of connections an actor has and the chances of that actor accessing new information are lower than when the actor is situated at the intersection of two separate networks; Ronald Burt (1992) called these network-linking phenomena "structural holes." However, network theory says nothing about strategies for the gatekeeping of information, so widespread in highly competitive environments. Moreover, network analysis makes the chances for success dependent on an individual's access to information, at the cost of other variables, such as reputation-building (or various modes of accumulating symbolic capital). Nevertheless, although network theory is incompatible with field theory from the point of view of its presuppositions, they can be made compatible if one considers network analysis as a method, rather than as a theory of the social world (see chapter II; also De Nooy [2003]).

Neither a direct expression of an era's worldview, nor the straightforward reflection of reality, literature circumvents the binary between rationalism and empiricism. Understood as the manifestation of the collective consciousness, of ideology, or of the structure of affects, literature is mediated by the social relations between classes or class fractions, whose contradictions it reflects. Conceived of as an act of communication, literature must be understood within the system of authorities that mediate it. Whether perceived via an institution, a system, a field, a world, or a network of relations, it is mediated by the social sphere that produces it. These mediations will be approached in the chapters that follow across three levels: the conditions of production of literary works, the sociology of literary works, and the sociology of reception.

II

The Social Conditions for
the Production of Literary Works

The conditions of production and the circulation of literary works are determined, first, by the relations that the political, economic, and religious powers maintain with respect to literature, and the social role they ascribe to it. These conditions depend, second, on the social recruitment of writers, on the conditions in which they work, and on their professional organization, as well as on the functioning of the world of letters and its institutions (academies, literary circles, literary prizes, journals).

The Situation of Literature in Society

The external constraints that bear upon cultural production are of two kinds, ideological and economic: on the one hand, the dominant ideology, which controls production via the intermediation of state and/or religious institutions; and, on the other, the market (Sapiro 2003a). The place of literature in society is also determined by the differentiation of social activities and the division of intellectual labor, and manifests itself in conceptions of the writer's social role.

The Ideological Control of Literature

From censorship to policies of support for literary creation and book production, the relationship of political power to literature across different political regimes offers a fertile terrain for research, which has been widely explored by historians and, increasingly, historians of literature. Depending on the regime, ideological control is enforced via the regulation of publication (censorship or legislation restricting freedom of expression, lists of bans, and so on), of economic exchange, and of professional organization. Added to this are the systems for rewarding and remunerating the most dedicated intellectuals. Archival records on censorship reveal the categories of judgment and the principles of classification used by the representatives of the state apparatus (regarding the case of South Africa under apartheid, see McDonald [2009]). Beyond censorship, nonliberal regimes (for instance, absolute monarchies, fascist and communist states, military dictatorships) are characterized by a strict centralization of the bodies in charge of circulating cultural products and of professional organizations. In communist regimes, over and above censorship, ideological control has been exercised via the writers' unions, in line with the model developed in the former Soviet Union (Garrard and Garrard [1990]; on the Romanian case, see Dragomir [2007]). The Egyptian Writers' Union was a key part of the Nasserite system of supervising and organizing writers, political control being accompanied by a certain liberalism on the artistic front (Jacquemond 2003/2008). From the French Revolution to the neoliberal policies of the second half of the twentieth century, the liberalization of economic exchange has often been associated with the claim of political liberalism (freedom of expression, freedom of association, and so on) and cultural liberalism (freedom of creation and consumption). In all cases, whether it be a question of repression or of prevention, ideological control depends not only on the system in place but also on the means of its application, which may be more or less strict (on modern China, see Hockx [2012, 2019]).

The system of control has both a direct and indirect impact on cultural production, ranging from explicit guidelines, as in the case of socialist realism (Robin 1986/1992), to self-censorship, to double-coded language. The manuscripts of Flaubert's *Madame Bovary* reveal, for example, the operative suppression of overly vulgar words like "whore" and "brothel," and of licentious images, blasphemies, and political allusions (Leclerc 1991, 199). The constraints, moreover, are not limited to legal sanctions: there are also social sanctions against violations of good taste, "public morality," and so forth. In nonliberal regimes, cultural supply thus appears largely determined by the ideological demands of the dominant fractions.

The systems of censorship and control often induce the practice of double-coded language, impelling people to read between the lines or to decipher the code (on the period of the German occupation in France, see Sapiro [1999/2014]; on the Spanish case, Bouju [2002]; and on the Egyptian case, Jacquemond [2003]). They also give rise to the development of underground publication networks, studies of which have looked at eighteenth-century France (Darnton 1982, 1991, 1995, 1996), the years of the German occupation in France (Sapiro 1999/2014), and the communist regimes (Popa 2010, 2019). Such systems produce situations of literary exile that can lead to the renewal of national fields of production (Jeanpierre 2004).

The Social Role of the Writer

The conditions of production contribute, moreover, to defining the social role of the writer, who embodies one of the principal mediations between works and external factors. The repression of cultural activities may have brought about, as a kind of backlash, the affirmation of the foundational values of autonomy and the redefinition of the writer's role according to intellectual values.

The literary and artistic fields asserted their autonomy with respect to the field of ideological production by the dissociation of the beautiful from the useful, a stance rooted in the Kantian theory of aesthetic judgment as disinterested judgment, and in the idea of *Beau idéal* (ideal beauty), of which the theory of *l'art pour l'art* (art for art's sake) is a radical expression (Heinrich Heine was its spokesman in Germany, Théophile Gautier in France [Cassagne 1997]). If, in the context of the Industrial Revolution, Romanticism promoted the ideal of beauty and exalted the power of the imagination (Williams 1983, 30–48), Realism adopted the value of objectivity from the scientific paradigm that was gaining cultural ground. To paint reality objectively and therefore truthfully thus became an artistic value that, like the ideal of beauty, shielded cultural productions from ethical judgment: the nineteenth-century realist writers (Flaubert, Zola, Descaves) brandished their realism as a defense against the accusations of contempt for public morality to which they were subjected (Leclerc 1991; Sapiro 2011b; on the notion of realism and its uses, see Boschetti [2014]). In this sense, the struggle against political control with regard to cultural production has contributed to the elaboration of the principles and values on which the relative autonomy of the literary field is based. This is why, in nonliberal regimes, the defense of autonomy is often associated with a political struggle to which it remains subordinate. Thus, under fascist or communist regimes, telling the truth in the midst of lies became a profession of faith for dissident authors like Bertolt Brecht in Germany and Paul Goma in Romania.

Since the nineteenth century, the figure of the writer has oscillated between that of the artist locked up in his ivory tower, like Flaubert, and that of the intellectual engaged in the world, like Zola or Sartre (on the latter, see Boschetti [1985/1988]; for a general overview of this idea, see Denis [2000]). Many works of social history and of the sociology of intellectuals have been devoted to the social conditions undergirding the political commitment of French writers during different conjunctures, such as the Paris Commune (Lidsky 1970), the Dreyfus Affair (Charle 1990/2015), the German occupation of France (Sapiro 1999/2014), and May 1968 (Gobille 2005a). These works differ from political histories of intellectuals in that they emphasize the relationship between the writers' political position-takings and their positions within the literary field. Political commitment has assumed various forms among writers, whether they be free intellectuals or subservient to institutions such as the Church (Serry 2004) or the Communist Party (Matonti 2005). Despite recurrent debates about the responsibility of the writer (Sapiro 2006a, 2007c, 2010b, 2010c, 2011b), a professional ideology has never been established around a code of ethics, as has occurred in other professions (for example, law and medicine).

Social Differentiation and Division of Intellectual Labor

Whereas the autonomization of the intellectual field took place on the basis of common values—such as truth, disinterestedness, and critical thinking—that allowed it to differentiate itself from the religious field (Masseau 1994), the nineteenth century was marked by what Andrew Abbott (1988) calls the "division

of expert labor" (see also Charle [1996]). This division participates in a more general process, described by Max Weber: the
differentiation of the spheres of life with the emergence of a body
of specialists who contribute to the institutionalization and autonomization of these spheres, as well as their separation from
laypersons. This process of monopolization can be more or less
advanced, depending on various factors: a higher or lower bar
of entry (academic training, academic qualifications, competitive examinations or entrance exams); the degree of homogeni-
zation within the profession, in terms of social recruitment and
the customs of practice; the existence of internal or external
competition; whether there is a monopoly on exclusive practice
(as was the case for physicians in France from 1892 onward);
and whether the professional organizations and their power
to impose rules on the body of specialists have been officially
recognized.

This division of labor had consequences for the spheres that
had encompassed these intellectual activities in the preceding
phase: as had previously been the case with the religious field,
the literary field was dispossessed of certain domains of activity
that were previously within its purview—for example, history,
psychology, and ethics—and that were, from the mid-nineteenth
century onward, monopolized by new professions whose expertise was recognized by the state (historians, psychologists,
sociologists, criminologists, and so on). This evolution helps to
explain the politicization of the literary field, and has generated
a conservative reaction within it (Sapiro 2003b, 2009a). This
reaction, in turn, partly accounts (notably because of the literary field's opposition to the scientific paradigm) for the affinities
and tensions between the literary and Catholic religious fields
in France from the end of the nineteenth century (Serry 2004).

Processes of differentiation are generally bolstered by the division of powers. The emergence in seventeenth-century France

of a new category of symbolic producers, men of letters, who distinguished themselves from the university *doctes*[1] by the use of vernacular French rather than Latin and by the valorization of a culture of entertainment rather than of erudition, took place with the support of the absolute monarchy, which aimed to bring about the linguistic unification of the kingdom (Viala 1985). The official establishment of the Académie Française in 1635 consecrated the delegation of linguistic power to writers, in return for their service to the king; autonomy with respect to the religious field thus implied submission to state power (Jouhaud 2000). The case of Egypt in the twentieth century illustrates the fluctuations of state power between support for writers' claims to autonomy from the religious field in return for their political submission, and concessions made to the Islamic authorities, who were represented in state institutions (Jacquemond 2003/2008).

The Logic of the Market

In the same way, whereas the rise of the book market constituted a counterpower that enabled intellectual producers to gradually escape state control and patronage (Bourdieu 1971a/1985b; Darnton 1982), the liberalization of the circulation of print—as well as the industrialization of its production in the nineteenth century—led to writers' increased dependence on consumer demand (Charle 1979). Forms like the serial novel allowed them to adjust to this demand, which could sometimes be gauged in readers' fan mail, and which would come to influence the works of authors such as Eugène Sue (Thiesse 1980).

This is why, according to Bourdieu (1971a/1985b, 1992/1996; 1993b, 112–41), the autonomy of the literary field asserted itself in the second half of the nineteenth century by claiming the primacy of peer and specialist judgment over that of laypeople. Against what the literary critic Sainte-Beuve called, in 1839, "industrial literature," which is situated at the pole of large-scale production and governed by the economic logic of short-term profitability, a pole of small-scale (or restricted) production was formed, which pronounced the irreducibility of the aesthetic value of a work to its market value. This aesthetic value is certified not only by peer judgment but also by intermediaries: publishers, critics, and consecrating authorities (such as literary prize juries).

The affirmation of the autonomy of aesthetic judgment with respect to economic, political, and moral expectations marked the advent of a relatively autonomous literary field, of which the theory of "art for art's sake" was the most extreme expression. The functioning of the literary world, like that of the other artistic spheres, rests, therefore, on the denegation of the economy. This is what constitutes the specificity of the economy of symbolic goods, inherited from a precapitalist model. The role of the publisher is all the more important, here, for its remit is to create not only the market value of the works but also their symbolic value. The publisher has the power to consecrate authors—to establish them as such—and to produce a belief in the value of the work by affixing the publisher's "brand" upon it, as in haute couture (Bourdieu 1977/1980). This magical power of consecration depends in turn on the symbolic capital accumulated by the publisher or, one might add, on other kinds of intermediaries (for example, literary agents, especially in the United Kingdom and the United States).

The sociology of literature thus leads to a sociology of publishing, which, in spite of the place ascribed to it by Robert Escarpit and Raymond Williams in their respective work (see chapter I), and unlike the booming field of book history, has only been in development since the end of the 1990s, following the research carried out by Pierre Bourdieu (1999a/2008) on the transformations of contemporary publishing in France. Bourdieu's study demonstrates the increasing weight of economic constraints on the book market as a result of consolidation and financialization in an era of globalization. State policies were introduced to support literary creation and publication in order to counterbalance the effects of this weight and to protect creators (Sapiro 2003a). The study of these policies raises the question of writers' social status (Sapiro and Gobille 2006; Sapiro 2019) and opens up comparative perspectives on the status of literature and of the writer in different countries (on Algeria, see Leperlier [2019]).

There is a lack of similar surveys that would allow us to assess the current state of literary publishing in other regions of the world (on Germany, see Tommek and Bogdal [2012]; Tommek [2015]). However, sociological and ethnographic studies of the publishing process are developing (see Thompson [2010] and Box 3; Childress [2019]). Research on literary agents is also burgeoning (Cottenet 2017; McGrath 2021; Sapiro and Leperlier 2021). Meanwhile, the mode of operation of the pole of large-scale production, governed by bestseller lists and serialization, has been studied in the case of Quebec (Saint-Jacques et al. 1994). In postcolonial contexts, the book industry in "central" languages, such as English and French, is still dominated by the large conglomerates based in those centers; this dependency conditions the production of literary and scholarly works and the access to international visibility (on India, see Narayanan 2012; on Francophone sub-Saharan Africa, Ducournau 2017).

The World of Letters and Its Institutions

Beyond the conditions of production, the sociology of literature has been concerned with the social recruitment of writers. That said, the professional development of the writer's trade is a vast and still largely unexplored field. It hinges upon the specialization of authors, the emergence of specific authorities, and recog-

Box 3. Changes in Literary Publishing in the United States and the United Kingdom

Also drawing on Bourdieu's work, John Thompson's (2010) ethnographic study of recent changes in the world of for-profit publishing in the United States and Great Britain identifies three main factors that explain the transformations in publishing practices since the 1970s: the growth of bookstore chains, the increased role of agents, and the consolidation and internationalization of large corporations. The exponential growth in production—in 2007, about 50,000 new fiction titles were published in the United States, twice as many as in 2003—in a period when potential readership is declining has led companies to refocus their efforts on what they consider to be "big books," that is, those with a very high sales potential. Two types of publications help reduce the uncertainty produced by debuting new authors: books by brand-name authors such as Stephen King, John Grisham, or Patricia Cornwell, and "long-sellers," books that continue to play a considerable, though sometimes small, role, which varies greatly from one publisher to another. In the face of consolidation at all levels (production, marketing, distribution), and thanks to lower costs of entry into the business, the number of small publishing houses has multiplied, reinforcing the polarization of the publishing field according to a dual economy (Thompson 2010).

nition by the state. One of the characteristics of the literary field, in contrast with its weak professionalization, is the multiplicity of sites of diffusion (reviews and publishing houses) and consecration. These authorities, which generally function as gatekeepers in the absence of a regulated right of entry (for instance, status or diploma), constitute so many variables from which the objective structure of the literary field can be grasped, by means of multiple correspondence analysis (MCA). The method of network analysis, for its part, enables us to understand the structure of relations and to measure reputations.

The Social Recruitment of Writers

Michel Foucault (1994/1999) dates the appearance of the "author function" to the sixteenth century, when the 1551 Edict of Chateaubriant made it compulsory in France to affix the name of the author and that of the printer to all publications. In this period, the number of authors multiplied in France as in England: from 86 English authors between 1501 and 1525 to 615 between 1576 and 1600 (Genêt 2002). Only in the following century did a sphere of specifically literary activity begin to differentiate itself in France, becoming autonomous in the nineteenth century (Viala 1985; Bourdieu 1992).

In the absence of regulations governing the conditions of access to the writing profession, and given that literary activity is often not the principal source of a writer's income, the population of authors is difficult to define and is characterized by its vague contours. Various criteria have been deployed to delineate it: publications, affiliations with literary institutions, awards won, and sociability networks. But the variations of criteria from one study to another make comparisons difficult (for an overview, see Sapiro [2007b]).

Several large surveys have tried to circumscribe the population of literary authors in France in the seventeenth, eighteenth, and nineteenth centuries: Alain Viala (1985) has established a population of 559 writers living and having published between 1643 and 1665, the moment of the "birth of the writer." Daniel Roche (1988) conducted a prosopography of the members of the French provincial academies in the seventeenth and eighteenth centuries. Robert Darnton (1992) compiled three cohorts of au-

thors from three editions of *La France littéraire* dating from
1757 (n = 1,187), 1769 (n = 2,367), and 1784 (n = 2,819). James
Smith Allen (1981) identified 560 literary authors active between
1820 and 1841. Rémy Ponton (1977) established a population of
616 writers active in France between 1850 and 1900 (born between 1820 and 1870).

Writers constituted an elite group by virtue of their social
origins and their secondary school education at a time when the
schooling rate was very low (between 1887 and 1926, it rose from
2.9 percent to 6.5 percent per age group). In the second half of
the nineteenth century, as in the first half of the twentieth, they
most often came from the upper or middle classes of the private
sector and from the intellectual bourgeoisie (Ponton 1977; Sapiro
1999, 706–7, 713/2014, 554–55, 562). At the turn of the century,
from the point of view of their social origins, they occupied an
intermediate position between the higher civil servants and the
elite academics of the Parisian establishments (Charle 1982; see
also Charle [1977] for a social geography of the Parisian literary
field comparing the writers' places of residence to those of the
other fractions of the dominant class). The regionalist writers,
who were mainly recruited from the middle and lower-middle
classes, were less endowed with inherited capital than their colleagues who had gained national recognition (Thiesse 1991). This
group was also differentiated by its almost exclusively provincial geographical origins; surveys conducted on a national scale
reveal the significance of geographical centralization for access
to the world of letters. The retreat into identity thus appears to
be linked to a process of relegation. This is also revealed in the
case of Catholic writers who, at the beginning of the twentieth
century, were moreover characterized by their education in private Catholic schools, whereas the majority of writers active at
that time were educated in public schools (Serry 2004).

The world of letters is also a site where gender inequalities and divides can be observed. If, contrary to the organized trades and professions, writing is an activity that has always been open to women with cultural capital, access to publication and especially to literary recognition is a relatively recent phenomenon. Although more and more women published their writings under the *ancien régime*, intellectual activities remained, for the vast majority of them, practices that had to be hidden or minimized under threat of being stigmatized or mocked as "silly, precious ladies" (*précieuses ridicules*). Excluded from the learned pole of the intellectual world, women were nevertheless to play an increasingly central role in high society, where the sociability of the salons and networks of correspondence reigned, while concealing their intellectual pretensions. The development of the book market in the nineteenth century triggered an increase in publications by women, but the redefinition of the boundaries between public and private spaces helped to bring about new forms of exclusion (Racine and Trebitsch 2004). If one estimates the number of women writing at the end of the nineteenth century at more than 700, it was, for society women (*les femmes du monde*), more an amateur than a professional activity; or, for the writers from modest backgrounds at the opposite pole, a lucrative job (Planté 1989; Saint Martin 1990). Preferring sometimes to camouflage themselves beneath a male identity, women writers in the nineteenth century confined themselves to writing devotional literature (for Maison de la Bonne Presse), children's literature, or the popular novel. Those who gained recognition generally came from the aristocracy or the bourgeoisie, unless they established themselves through scandal, like Colette, a typical product of upward social mobility through education who started out as her first husband Willy's ghostwriter before setting out on her own.

In 1904—following the foundation of the Prix Goncourt, and as a form of protest against the misogyny of its jurors, who would not award the prize to a woman until 1945—women writers, long excluded from institutional consecration, founded the Prix Femina, which rewards both men and women authors. This prize did not, however, prevent the exclusion of interwar women writers from the French literary canon: in the most selective anthologies, one finds at most six of them: Anna de Noailles, Rachilde, Colette, Nathalie Sarraute, Simone Weil, and Marguerite Yourcenar. In encyclopedic handbooks, their numbers range from 14 to 239, but they remain vastly underrepresented compared to their male peers (1:8), and they are grouped together as if forming a homogeneous entity (Milligan 1996). This segregation is one of the forms of exclusion engendered by the literary canon, which presents women writers as exceptions. It is also at work in the treatment of their literary output, which denies them the universality accorded to their male peers (the qualities they are granted are considered feminine, namely, their natural penchant for writing on love, kinship with nature, sensitivity, sensuality, and so on) and assigns them to two genres, autobiography and "romance." The accession of women to secondary and higher education has greatly altered this situation. The feminization of the literary field after World War II, especially since the 1970s, has been one of its most significant transformations. This has involved, above all, greater access to visibility and to consecration, even as the social and cultural competition remains harder for women than for their male peers, and forms of relegation and stigmatization remain (Naudier 2000). These conditions are even more difficult for women from the Maghreb, even as the francophone sphere has opened up a space of possibles for some of them, allowing them to emancipate themselves from the specific constraints that have burdened them in their countries of origin (Détrez 2012).

Regarding the contemporary period in France, Bernard Lahire and Géraldine Bois conducted a survey of 503 writers by questionnaire, based on two criteria: first, the publication of a work of literature (including self-publishing), as a deliberately broad indicator of literary activity in order to study its boundaries; second, an association with the Rhône Alpes region (this was due to the terms of the survey's financing) (Lahire 2006). These criteria induce biases that affect the general thesis on the weak professionalization of literary activity and on literature as a second profession: the choice of a nonrestrictive criterion (book publication) leads to an underestimation of the share of writers living from their pen and of the process of professionalization mentioned above, while the geographical criterion poses the problem of the representativeness of the population studied with respect to a national literary field that is centralized around the capital. Like those concerning previous periods, this survey nevertheless reveals the qualities necessary for access to recognition, in terms of both social origin (one-third of the authors in the population are children of upper-management professionals and members of the higher intellectual professions, and one-fifth are children of middle-management professions), and educational and cultural capital (more than 80 percent of the most literarily and nationally recognized writers have had at least two years of postsecondary education; the same percentage claims that they read more than twenty books per year). The study also provides data on production (number of books published, publishers represented, literary genres deployed, involvement in journals, translations, media reception, and so forth), writing conditions (time devoted to writing, space, commissions, and so on), membership in authors' societies and other professional bodies, participation in literary circles, and the relationship between these variables and the degree and type of recognition obtained, as well as one's self-identification as a writer. The question of the self-identification of contemporary writers is also treated, in a more qualitative manner, by Nathalie Heinich (2000).

The social selection performed by the literary field is even stricter for writers of foreign origin, especially when they come from former colonies, as revealed by Claire Ducournau's (2017) prosopographical survey of 151 writers from sub-Saharan Africa who have gained recognition since decolonization: the entry fee is much higher for these writers in terms of economic and cultural capital, and even more so for women than for men.

Professional Development of the Writing Trade

Few studies have focused on the forms of professional organization of the writing trade. The sociology of professions has overlooked this activity, which, like creative activities in general, represents a "challenge for sociological analysis" (Freidson 1986): unlike the organized professions, creative activities are weakly regulated; there are no predetermined entry requirements to access them, nor is there any specific training, although creative writing curricula and workshops have come to play a significant role in building literary careers in the United States and are developing in other places (McGurl 2009; Bedecarré 2017); and they do not ensure a regular income for the majority of those who practice them. Nevertheless, creative trades cannot be reduced to a pastime, or to a "game" as some suggest (Lahire 2006), because individual investment in them is so total, and social belief in them so strong. Yet despite its weak regulation, one can observe, historically speaking, that the writing trade underwent a process of "professional development"—in the sense of Abbott (1988), who proposes this term to avoid the teleological connotation of "professionalization." The relevant professional organizations (authors' societies and associations) and the legal frameworks concerning the material conditions of the writer's profession (copyright, grants-in-aid, social security, retirement, and so on) provide two angles from which to approach the trade (Sapiro and Gobille 2006; Sapiro 2019).

The first embryo of a professional organization in France, the Society of Dramatic Authors, was created by Beaumarchais in 1777, the same year that the *droit d'auteur* (authors' property rights over their work) was recognized by royal decree—though this right applied only to books and not to theatrical adaptations. During the Revolution, it was notably in response to demands made by playwrights that authors' rights were consecrated under the Le Chapelier (1791) and Lakanal (1793) laws (Hesse 1990).[2] Many of the struggles led by writers in the nineteenth century aimed at expanding these rights, both in time (extension of the right of heirs *post mortem*) and in space (international recognition of literary property), and to media other than books (the theater, newspapers, audiovisual media, and, today, digital media).

Founded in 1838 by Honoré de Balzac and Louis Desnoyers to promote the "material and moral dignity of writers" through the reaffirmation and protection of literary property, the Société des Gens de Lettres (SGDL) fought to defend the interests of writers against the press, where literary property did not apply as such, and where forgery and plagiarism were on the rise. This struggle was internationalized with the 1878 Brussels International Literary Congress. The SGDL also helped draft the Berne Convention, the first international convention on literary and artistic property, signed in 1886 and revised several times since. This effort at universal harmonization has not resolved, although it has reduced, the gap between the French conception of literary proprety (*droit d'auteur*), which privileges the author's moral rights, namely the right of publication, the right to the respect of the work's integrity, and the right of withdrawal, over patrimonial or pecuniary rights (moral rights remain inalienable since they belong to the persona), and American copyright, which conceives of the work as a good that is subject to economic law.

More broadly, the writers' ambivalent status results from the multiple ways in which literary works may be considered—as goods, as fruits of labor, or as a service—according to the different groups and bodies that contribute to their production and valorization on the market: authors, publishers, booksellers, critics, the public, and the state. The different interpretations of literary property thus reflect writers' fluctuation among several social statuses. As owners of their works, they may print and sell them for their own benefit, or grant to a third party the right to sell them. In the latter case, however, they resemble more workers paid for the fruits of their labors, although the intellectual dimension of writing differentiates them from manual workers, and places them within the category of services. They also differ from salaried workers in their autonomy and their responsibility with regard to their audience, much as with liberal professions. These different conceptions, which entail their own respective fiscal systems and social protection rights, have appeared in particular historical contexts, and their relative importance has varied as power relations between groups of actors have evolved. While the predominant conception in the first half of the nineteenth century in France was that authors were owners of their work, changes in writers' work conditions—particularly the development of capitalism in publishing—and the struggle to obtain social benefits led some of them in the interwar period to lay claim to the status of "intellectual workers." This was, however, ultimately a losing effort, put down after the wars (Sapiro and Gobille 2006).

The 1960s were a time of intense reflection on the socioprofessional conditions of the writer's trade, which came as literary authority was being contested by students (Gobille 2018). In this period, with the development of new media and storage technologies, the notion of the author of the written word was extended to include writers, scriptwriters, multimedia authors and writers on the internet. If one can speak of a process of professionalization of the writer's trade, it remains unfinished, in particular with respect to the recognition of social rights—as shown by a survey conducted on the economic conditions of writing in France in the 1970s (Vessilier-Ressi 1982), the results of which, however, are incomplete.

Beyond the production and publication of literary works, literary careers are organized around related activities (such as, traditionally, translation, adaptation, and participation on prize juries) that participate, to varying degrees, in both the symbolic and professional recognition of writers, alongside literary prizes. Among these activities, literary events (for instance, festivals, public readings) and residencies (some of them state-funded, others affiliated with private initiatives) have grown in importance since the 1990s and continue to offer writers new forms of visibility, networking, and career opportunities (Sapiro and Rabot 2017; Sapiro 2019; see also chapter IV). Creative writing programs also offer opportunities for established writers to teach and thus participate in the professional development of the writing trade.

The Institutions of Literary Life

Weakly regulated, literary life is characterized by the multiplicity of authorities that contribute to the definition of literature: training and socialization bodies (high schools, universities, specialized schools, and so on), sites of sociability (salons, literary circles, cafés), organs of production and dissemination (journals, publishers, press outlets, libraries), consecrating authorities (prizes, academies, societies devoted to preserving the legacy of an author), professional organizations (authors' societies, associations, unions), literary groups or schools—all of which can be taken as objects of study.[3] The multiplicity of more or less institutionalized forms of group-formation that play the role of consecrating or self-legitimizing authorities stands in contrast to the absence of a monopolistic institution such as exists in the religious field for the major monotheistic religions (the Church), or in the organized professions (professional bodies or *ordres*). The weak codification of the writer's profession reinforces the importance of these consecrating bodies as regulatory authorities of literary life. They are, moreover, "places of dialogue and conflict between the literary space and the political, financial and religious powers" (Viala 1988).

For studying the seventeenth century, Viala (1985, 215–16) proposes modeling writers' strategies for navigating between different spaces of recognition, such as clienteles, salons, academies, and patrons. He also tracks how the various modes of legitimation have transformed over time, with the decline of private academic societies coming to the benefit of the official academies studied by Daniel Roche (1988). Meanwhile, from the eighteenth century onward, the salons came to occupy an important place in literary sociability and in defining the dominant taste (Lilti 2005/2015).

Despite the rise of the market, the academies continued to play a role in the hierarchization of the French literary world, alongside other literary authorities, such as journals and prizes (Sapiro 2016c). The latter acquired new visibility with the creation of the Prix Goncourt in 1903 and, from the mid-1920s onward, became more relevant to publishers because of their growing impact on sales. Converting symbolic capital into economic capital, prizes now play a decisive role in literary life (on this "economy of prestige," see English [2008]). The principal literary authority of the English-speaking literary space, the Booker Prize, has been increasingly market-oriented: Todd

(1996) speaks of a "kind of commercial canon," and Norris (2006, 155) analyzed the Booker's "conflation of literary merit and sales potential." Winning the Booker Prize significantly enhances an author's chance of having their work translated into other languages, at least since the beginning of the 1980s (Pickford 2011). Like the Nobel, it can be defined as an institution that participates in the making of world literature (Helgesson and Vermeulen 2015) and of world authorship (Braun et al. 2020).

Comparing the sociological profiles of the members of different literary institutions, such as the Académie Française and the Académie Goncourt, enables us to grasp the types of dispositions that prevail in one or the other (Sapiro 1999/2014). On the one hand, the Académie Française is distinguished by the importance of civil servants[4] among its coopted membership (from the point of view of their origins as well as the professions they have practiced), which is consistent with its status as a state institution. On the other hand, the strong presence of men of letters living by their pens in the Académie Goncourt reflects the will of its two founders to distance themselves from the enlightened amateurism of the older Académie Française by coopting only professionalized writers—and thus marking a stage in the process of professionalization. Meanwhile, the low overall educational capital of its members and the absence of teachers from its ranks echo the competitive struggle that pitted writers against professors under the Third Republic (Sapiro 1999/2014).

These authorities carry out a form of social selection that results in the exclusion of writers from dominated (or subaltern) groups. The election of the first woman *académicienne*, Marguerite Yourcenar, in 1980, provoked violent confrontations between her opponents, for whom the entry of a woman into the Académie Française was inconceivable, and her advocates, who, with the support of the government of Valéry Giscard d'Estaing and a large part of the media, intended to subvert the academic tradition (Naudier 2004). Three years later, in 1983, under the socialist government of François Mitterrand, Leopold Sédar Senghor became the first writer of African origin to be elected to the Académie (on the stakes of his election, see Ducournau [2017]).

If their existence testifies to the relative autonomization of literary activity, these authorities can also become vehicles of heteronomy in the field, especially in times of crisis. Thus, during the German occupation of France, the Académie Française and the Académie Goncourt served as instruments for imposing political constraints, leading opposition writers to organize themselves and, in some cases, to join the intellectual Resistance (Sapiro 1999/2014).

As in the scientific field, the site of authority most representative of the principle of autonomy is the journal or review, a place where criticism and peer judgment can be exercised without external constraints. Thanks to political liberalization, journals proliferated in France under the Third Republic. However, the unprecedented expansion of the intellectual professions and of the printed word at the end of the nineteenth century (Charle 1979) raised the problem of survival for these small, fragile enterprises, which were doomed to collapse in the absence of resources. Often financed thanks to the personal fortune of one of their leaders, they depended closely on the total abnegation of a select few, and favored the personalization of social relations within a strongly individualized literary field.

By associating itself with a publishing house, the Symbolist review *Le Mercure de France* inaugurated an original model to perpetuate its enterprise and to allow the review's contributors to publish their works in book form (Boschetti 1991). This model was adopted by other reviews, the paradigmatic example being *La Nouvelle Revue française (NRF)*, which gave birth to the Gallimard publishing house. However, even if these magazines maintained, in relation to the houses they founded, their "show-case" role and their authority of consecration, their association with a commercial enterprise required a compromise between aesthetic demands and the interests of the publishing house, as the history of the *NRF* demonstrates (Sapiro 1999, 377–466/2014, 293–361).

The borders of the literary field and its margins have also been the object of sociological investigation: a set of parallel entities "in imitation" of those in the field constitute "universes of consolation" for the pretenders excluded from the circles of legitimate consecration (Poliak 2006).

Structure of the Literary Field and MCA

Unlike the notion of the profession, which presupposes the unity and homogeneity of a group, the concept of the field makes it possible to grasp the principles of structuration governing relatively autonomous spaces of intellectual or cultural activity, which constitute a mediation between the political and economic constraints and the works produced in those spaces. One of the principles of polarization that runs through these spaces is the opposition between the dominants and the dominated, an opposition that refers back to the trade's working conditions (Bourdieu 1979/1984b). Often intersecting with the opposition between "veterans" and "newcomers," the dominant-dominated polarity also reflects social differences; for example, in the eighteenth-century world of letters, the social differences between writers who held seats in the academies and public posts, and those condemned to live by their pen—the practitioners of "gutter Rousseauism" (*les Rousseau du ruisseau*) whom Voltaire called the "literary scum [*la canaille littéraire*]" (Darnton 1985, 35).

But the world of letters also witnessed the emergence, beginning under the *ancien régime*, of an opposition between a heteronomous pole of "organic intellectuals," to use Gramsci's term, and a pole that claimed its autonomy from the political and religious powers by asserting its authority among the public. Later, with the development of the book market, many writers would claim their autonomy in the face of economic constraints.

These principles of structuration define a relational space of positions that is homologous, according to field theory, with the space of position-takings (Bourdieu 1992, 176/1996, 231). One of the most adequate statistical tools for grasping the structure of the literary field is multiple correspondence analysis (MCA), which proposes a geometric representation of relations obtained from a matrix formed by individuals (persons or institutions) and by a set of variables (Rouanet and Leroux 1993). If we are interested in social recruitment within the literary field, variables such as age, social origin, educational trajectory, membership in an avant-garde movement, collaboration with a particular journal or publisher, and so on constitute so many relevant properties. MCA brings together those writers who share the greatest number of properties and place at a distance those who have the least in common. The graph of variables portrays the distribution of properties and entities, and thus the structure of the field.

A survey of 185 French writers active between 1940 and 1944 included, in addition to social data, a set of variables on places of publication, publishers and journals, major prizes won, indices of short- and long-term recognition according to authors' inclusion in contemporary anthologies and dictionaries, literary genres deployed, and aesthetic and political stances taken, accounted for at different moments of the authors' careers. The result of the MCA (85 variables, 236 active modalities, and 12 illustrative modalities), according to the first factor, on the horizontal axis, contrasted the dominant pole with the dominated pole in terms of age (experienced writers vs. novices), literary genre (novelists vs. poets), and institutional consecration (literary prizes and membership in academies vs. small literary journals). The second factor, on the vertical axis, distinguished between writers with a high level of symbolic recognition, concentrated around Gallimard and the *NRF* (here we find the Nobel Laureates: Paul Valéry, André Gide, Roger Martin du Gard), and those marked by a lack of recognition, and whose presence in the field was due to their activity as magazine editors or critics. This latter pole is strongly politicized, in contrast to the writers most endowed with specific symbolic capital, who distanced themselves from politics. During the German occupation, the political positions taken in this space were distributed in a manner homologous to the structure of the field: whereas, on the first axis, the pole of worldly (*temporel*) domination was mostly in favor of the Vichy regime and collaboration, the literary Resistance was recruited from the dominated pole. The latter found sympathizers at the pole of symbolic recognition, who did not, however, go so far as to enter the Underground (Sapiro 1999/2014, 2002a).

In the same vein, a homology was shown between the political position-takings of the Algerian writers during the civil war of the 1990s and their position in the literary field—the dominant ones, endowed with international recognition, being more likely to oppose the Islamic party (which won the local elections in 1990) than the dominated ones, who joined the prodialogue camp (Leperlier 2019).

MCA can also be used to explore the various types of literary careers and modes of consecration: it reveals, for example, the impact of major Parisian publishers on the conditions governing access to recognition for writers from sub-Saharan Africa (Ducournau 2017).

The Structure of Relationships and the Measurement of Reputations: Network Analysis

While the notion of a network rightly attracts the interest of literary historians, a qualitative approach still prevails in the majority of empirical studies (De Marneffe and Denis 2006). Literary history nevertheless provides incomparably rich material for network analysis, which is still far from being harnessed as fully as it could be: writers' correspondence, critical reviews, social scenes, organs of diffusion. Network analysis seems particularly appropriate for exploring the universe of blurred and porous borders that is the world of letters, structured around micro-milieux (journals, for example) and around networks of informal relations, which often take the personalized form of elective affinities. In the absence of any regulated conditions of entry to the writing profession, social capital plays a very strong role in terms of gaining access to publication and forming literary reputations. Network analysis also provides a means of describing the structure of relations in these literary circles according to different types of connections (membership in groups or clubs, ties to publication venues, access to recognition, and so on).

Freed from interactionist presuppositions, and combined with field theory (see Box 3), network analysis thus proves to be a fruitful method for the sociology of literature (Sapiro 2006b). First, it allows us to explore the structure of the relations between groups or institutions in terms of hierarchization, the degree of segmentation, and the relationship between the center and the periphery. Network analysis also makes it possible to delineate the segmentation of the field by genre (poetry circles, theatrical milieux, and so on) or by literary schools, whose functioning in the form of "cliques" can be opposed to the more distended networks of journals and reviews, themselves connected by individuals who link networks by filling the "structural holes" between them (as defined by Burt [1992]). It provides, as well, a tool for measuring the degree of autonomy characterizing different forms of literary sociability: for example, the Goncourts' famous loft (*grenier*), where writers met and mingled among themselves, distinguished itself from the more worldly salons, where they mixed with the upper fractions of the dominant class.

The types of networks can be differentiated according to their degree of openness or closure (journals vs. the academies), their durability (institutions like the academies vs. the ephemeral networks behind manifestos or reviews of varying longevity), or their degree of institutionalization (institutions or associations possessing legal status vs. informal networks such as circles or coteries). But above all, network analysis makes it possible to link these different groups. It also offers perspectives for studying the relations between the literary field and other fields, for example, the political field, the journalistic field, the artistic field, the musical field, and so on. Finally, it offers a means of investigating exchanges between national fields—for example, via the system of relations between authors, publishers, and translators in the case of translated literature (for instance, French literature in the United States [Sapiro 2015c]), or between the center and the periphery of linguistic areas. In the latter case, for example, the organization of the Belgian literary subfield as a network has ensured its autonomy in relation to the Parisian center of the francophone literary space (Dozo 2011; Fréché 2009).

Beyond interactions between individuals, network analysis can be used to probe and model relationships of another kind, such as the correlation between, on the one hand, the "symbolic classifications" of authors (by critics) into schools or movements and, on the other, the material links between these authors established through publication in the same journals or with the same publishers (De Nooy 1991). Such uses of network analysis enable

Box 4. The Structure of the Literary Field in Cologne: Network Analysis and MCA

Can network analysis reveal the structure of the literary field? This was the question asked in a survey of a population of 222 writers living in and around Cologne, one of Germany's cultural centers (150 responses obtained). Four types of relationships were explored: familiarity with the work; friendship; help received; desired closeness (whom would you have invited to dinner?). That the questions concerned not only interactions but also familiarity with the work and relationship preferences breaks with the interactionist assumption of network theory. Using a statistical method, seven groups ("blockmodels") were identified according to the density of relationships: the cultural elite (n = 6), the organizational elite (5), the subelite (20), the first semiperiphery (22), the second semiperiphery (33), the local culture (10), the periphery (43). The lack of relations between the "blocks" was interpreted as a segmentation phenomenon; unequal relations as an indicator of hierarchy.

The structure of relations can be correlated with the type of capital that predominates. If economic capital is predominant, one can expect a structure of the literary field strongly hierarchized according to sales figures and weakly segmented into genres. If social capital predominates, the structure will tend to be divided

us to operationalize the idea of networks as coordinates for the positions occupied in the field (Klinkenberg 2006]).

The construction of literary reputation can also be approached via a combination of network analysis and regression analysis. One survey of contemporary French poets distinguishes between peer recognition and "renown," the process by which a poet leaves their inner circle to become known to the general public (S. Dubois 2009). The study shows that the passage from one to the other is not systematic, and it analyzes the into distinct and weakly hierarchical segments, institutionalized according to genres, professional associations, and so on.

If cultural capital predominates, the structure will be both strongly segmented and hierarchical, with an initial hierarchical segmentation between legitimate art and popular culture, and an internal hierarchy within the legitimate segment ordered by fame or renown.

The result of the network analysis showed a primary partition of the social structure of the Cologne literary field into two main segments, the center and the periphery, comprising 62 percent and 38 percent of the writers, respectively. But while the center is structured in a clearly hierarchical way, the periphery is characterized by the virtual absence of relations with the other blocks, which indicates strong segmentation. The periphery is itself segmented between a peripheral space, where internal relations are weak, and a very dense, self-enclosed island constituted by the regionalist writers. This highly segmented and hierarchical structure confirms the predominance of cultural capital over other types of capital, a finding corroborated by MCA. Social capital is less significant, with economic capital hardly mattering at all (Anheier et al. 1995).

cumulative effect of the indicators of renown (number of books with a major publisher, number of books in paperback, receiving the Grand Prix de Poésie, serving as president of the Centre National du Livre's poetry commission, inclusion in monographs, and so on), bringing out the "Matthew effect" (following Merton's expression to designate the effect of cumulative success) in the case of two poets: Yves Bonnefoy and Philippe Jaccottet. The reputation indicators for this population were later systematized (S. Dubois 2009; S. Dubois and François 2013).

The conditions of production and circulation of literary works reveal the external constraints (political, economic, and social) that weigh on literary activity, as well as the internal mechanisms of selection and consecration that govern it. To understand how these conditions are refracted in literary production, we must now turn to the sociology of literary works.

III

The Sociology of Literary Works

The sociology of literary works (*sociologie des oeuvres*) aims at overcoming the opposition between internal and external analysis, in order to understand how these works refract the social world. To this end, it performs a double rupture against, on the one hand, the Marxist tradition, which tends to relate artworks directly to the social conditions of production (theory of reflection; see chapter I), and, on the other hand, against the "biographical illusion" (Bourdieu 1986), which consists in imputing the work to the unique singularity of an individual. Writers do not create *ex nihilo*. Rather, they inscribe themselves in the space of representations and social discourses, and also in a structured space of possibles, which offers them genres, models, ways of acting—so many social facts specific to the world of letters, which vary in time and space. Once this space or these variations have been reconstructed, the next step is to understand the principles behind the choices made by different groups and individuals. The choices are partly determined by the social properties of the individuals (social origin, intellectual formation, ethical and aesthetic dispositions, and so on) and by the system of relations that they cultivate with their peers.

From Representations to Ways of Doing

If the classical definition of art and literature as the imitation of nature has been strongly challenged by modern aesthetic theories, the problem of representing the world continues to arise for writers, as well as for theorists, historians, and sociologists of literature. But beyond the fact that literature is not, any more than art, reducible to representation—as the case of poetry testifies— the problem of representing the world is, in the social sciences, too often dissociated from the problem of the *ways* of representing (or the refusal to represent), and from the particular point of view of the author or the artist. "Space of possibles" (Bourdieu), "repertoire" (Even-Zohar), "literary institutions" (Viala): different terms have been adopted to designate these ways of doing, which define "the literary" in a given sociohistorical configuration. The point of view of the author is also inscribed—even if as a means of distinguishing itself—in that of one or several groups or communities, whether national, religious, ethnic, class, or gender-based.

Literature and Social Representation(s)

Art history has long been interested in how works of art participate in the "worldview" (*Weltanschauung*) of a historical period. From the 1920s to the 1950s, this notion was at the heart of the sociology of literature, which offered a less idealistic and more socialized approach by linking *Weltanschauung* to social groups (see chapter I). Having fallen into disuse for reasons that should be studied,[1] the worldview perspective was first replaced, in the Marxist-inspired approaches of the 1960s and 1970s, by the concepts of "collective consciousness" and "ideology" (on the latter, see Eagleton [2007]). These concepts have been criticized in their turn, notably by Raymond Williams (1977), who preferred notions more apt to account for the incorporation of collective consciousness within individuals, such as "common sense," "structures of feeling," and "affects." For example, Williams (1983, 87–109) analyzes the way in which nineteenth-century English novels dealing with the social transformations of the Industrial Revolution ("industrial novels")—such as Elizabeth Gaskell's *Mary Barton* (1848) or Charles Dickens's *Hard Times* (1854)—attempt to reconstruct the experience and daily suffering of the working classes by arousing affective reactions of empathy or repulsion in the reader. In the 1980s, following the approach taken by Foucault, it was the notion of "representation" that became fashionable.

Coinciding with the rise of the history of representations, a study by the Québécois scholar Marc Angenot (1989) has shown that literary works convey the discourses that are widespread at the time of their production. Indeed, literary works participate in a wider discursive space from which they feed. The Naturalist writers of the nineteenth century drew descriptions of disease symptoms from popular medical textbooks, and theories of heredity provided them with a narrative framework of sociobiological causality. The harmful consequences of alcoholism were dramatized in Zola's *L'Assommoir* (1877), a great success at the time, and in Paul Bonnetain's *Charlot s'amuse* (1883), the story of an onanist who is the victim of a hereditary defect due to his father's alcoholism. Press archives offer fertile ground for studying these social discourses and their forms (Thérenty 2007).

The example of Naturalism reveals the authority that science had acquired by the end of the nineteenth century: the writers who claimed to be part of the movement took up scientific theses

without questioning them. One perceives the need to reconstitute the hierarchy of the discourses according to the authority
of the groups that produce them: clergy, men of the law, scien-
tists, doctors, psychologists, historians, sociologists, and so on.
In the same way that certain sciences, such as psychoanalysis,
have largely drawn on literary works, literature has always been
nourished by contemporary knowledge: Surrealism was imbued
with psychoanalysis; the College of Sociology, a group of writers
and researchers who gathered around Georges Bataille at the
end of the 1930s, drew on anthropological and sociological concepts (Hollier 1988/1995).

Conversely, literary works provide a source for studying the
social representations of a historical moment. With its sociological ambitions, Realist literature lends itself particularly well to
this exercise. Sociocriticism has attempted to bring these representations into relief in order to reconstitute the social universe
of the novel, whether in terms of social relations, spaces (for example, the city), or historical events (Duchet 1979; Zima 1985). Interesting perspectives have also been opened up by ethnographic
criticism, which sets the realist novelistic universe against the
mores and beliefs of the environments described therein (see
Jean-Marie Privat's study of *Madame Bovary* [1994]).

Class relations are a favorite subject for novelists, from Dickens and Stendhal to Céline, via Balzac, Austen, Flaubert, Zola,
Proust, Wharton, Dos Passos, and Aragon. What emerges from
their novels is a social philosophy, even a "sociological" vision of
the world, which can be reconstructed. Stendhal's novels all have
as their background the class struggle between the aristocracy
and the bourgeoisie that raged under the Bourbon Restoration
and then under the July Monarchy, his heroes always struggling
against the social determinisms in which they are caught. As
Jacques Dubois (2007) suggests, the resulting politicization of
romantic relations has as its counterpart the eroticization of

politics. The reversal of power relations between the aristocracy and the bourgeoisie under the Third Republic is at the heart of Proust's *À la recherche du temps perdu* (*In Search of Lost Time*). To a now declining nobility, pulled down by its decaying fractions in spite of its efforts to hold on to its rank, is opposed an ascendant and soon triumphant bourgeoisie, whose subdivisions Proust studies—from the uppermost fraction, which ends up allying itself with the old aristocracy of the Boulevard Saint-Germain, to the cultured fraction, which claims a distinction not of birth but of superior taste in the arts.[2] Implementing the sociological theory of Gabriel Tarde, of whom he was an admirer, Proust shows that the retreat of the nobility into its traditions and privileges causes it to lose its example-setting role, which once encouraged the other classes to imitate it, and leads to its downfall (Dubois 1997). The rival salons constitute an ideal laboratory for observing these competing strategies of distinction (Bidou 1997). But the scene for the social mingling that disrupts all points of reference is the beach, which is overtaken by the middle and lower-middle class eager for thrills and devoted to sports (Dubois 1997). This class is embodied by the figure of Albertine, Marcel's great love, who unwittingly betrays the ethos of her class. Captured in an impressionistic mode, which escapes a fixed point of view, she "upsets the narrative logic," compromising the deterministic structure of the novel (Dubois 1997, 76, our translation).

First seized upon by feminist critics, gender is a productive prism for exploring the worldviews conveyed in literary works (see Box 5). Among the countless publications that deal with gendered representations in literature, I will focus here on those that use gender as a framework for studying social relations according to a clearly sociological perspective.

In works with sociological ambitions, such as those of Balzac, gender relations offer a fertile ground for exploring the articu-

Box 5. Gender Relations in Virginia Woolf's *To The Lighthouse*

Bourdieu's analysis of gender relations in Virginia Woolf's *To The Lighthouse* reveals the partition of male and female points of view by contrasting the father's speech (*parole*), which expresses a realism complicit with the world order, triggering his son's hatred, with the mother's speech, which embodies contingency based on the act of faith. At the same time, the analysis reveals a feminine complicity with masculine domination, which allows the father of the family to exercise his power in spite of flaws that Mrs. Ramsay is not blind to and that she strives to hide from those around her— for example, in the ironic episode where he is seen reciting lines from Tennyson's "The Charge of the Light Brigade," which stages the *illusio* of the *libido dominandi* that Mr. Ramsay performs for lack of having materialized it in his academic career (Bourdieu 1998b, 76–86).

lations between affective relations, social forms of sexuality, and social order, at a transformative time for the legal system and its laws concerning property and the family (Lucey 2003). Sexual binarism and the masculine/feminine hierarchy were being upset by a whole literary tradition that had put a spotlight on the figures of the lesbian and the emancipated woman, two incarnations of the third sex aspiring to escape from male domination, and of which Théophile Gautier's *Mademoiselle de Maupin* (1835) and George Sand's *Gabriel* (1840) provide paradigmatic examples, at a time when inversion and transvestism were considered pathological (Murat 2006). Conversely, in a society that assigned men a productive function, intellectual activity, which was relegated to the domain of the sensitive, the dreamy, the frivolous, the unproductive, the passive, and the impotent, could be experienced as a form of feminization, the mark of which can be seen in works ranging from Swiss author Henri-

Frédéric Amiel's diary to the writings of Brazilian disciples of the French writer Anatole France (Boltanski 1975; Miceli 1975; see also Sapiro [2007b]).

The appropriation of discourses on gender and the female body was at the heart of the feminist revolution of the 1970s, blurring the boundaries between the sexes (Naudier 2000). Similarly, representations of sexuality in the works of women writers from the Maghreb reveal the taboos of a society in which virginity is still a paramount issue of family honor, from the experience of the wedding night itself as rape to the raping of virgins by warriors under the guise of "pleasure marriages" (Charpentier 2013).

Sociologists have also explored social representations and the ideological dimensions at work in the spy novel (Neveu 1985), the detective novel (Collovald and Neveu 2004), and the romantic novel (Radway 1984; Péquignot 2001). From a different perspective, exploring science fiction has enabled Marxist critic Fredric Jameson (2005) to grasp the utopian potential of this genre (in Philip K. Dick's novels, for instance).

Together with interpretative methods, quantitative analyses (lexicometry, network analysis, algorithms, and so on), and cartography offer tools to explore literary works. Pierre Bourdieu (1992, 23/1996, 6) thus proposes a map of the geographical structure of the novelistic space in Flaubert's *L'Éducation sentimentale* (*Sentimental Education*), from which the structure of the field of power can be grasped. Franco Moretti (1997) has systematized this approach as a method for exploring literary works in his *Atlas of the European Novel*, showing, among other things, that the different subgenres of the novel—the gothic novel, the sentimental novel, the novel of ideas, the historical novel—are distinguished by their respective spatial configurations. This configuration evolves under the effect of social transformations, such as industrialization and the formation of nation-states, as the analysis of the geographical space of village narratives in Great Britain and Germany in the first quarter of the nineteenth century reveals (Moretti 2005, 48–50). Moretti has also used network analysis to study seventeenth-century tragedies. By measuring the density of exchanges between characters, it is possible to analyze their position within a network (degree of centrality and intermediation), and to reveal the structure of the relations between them. This method provides a tool useful for comparisons among works and among countries.

Literature as Practical Knowledge

The relationship between literature and "worldview" or contemporary social representations cannot be reduced to a matter of simple reflection. Literature itself plays a role in the "framing" of reality, to use a concept drawn from sociologist Erving Goffman's (1974) study of the social frames of experience. Fredric Jameson has theorized how narratives frame the perception and memory of historical events (Jameson 1981). To understand this framing function, we must abandon the simplistic schema of representation and of the greater or lesser adequacy of the fictional world to reality—not that these issues are irrelevant, but they risk missing the essential point, namely, how literature participates in the "worldview" of a historical period, or even in its "knowledge" (Sapiro 2023). The French philosopher Jacques Bouveresse thus proposes that we consider literature as a form of "practical knowledge" (Bouveresse 2008, 63–64).

The notion of exemplarity appears, in this respect, more adequate than that of representation to think through the cognitive function of literature, between representativeness or typicality, on the one hand, and models or rules of action, on the other. The process of typification thus characterizes Realist exemplarity, according to the model established by Balzac (David 2010). The research undertaken by the Groupe φ (Bouju et al. 2007) explores the above notions from three angles: first the links between exemplification—concrete cases and instances—and exemplarity, which raise the problem of the conditions of generalization; next, the relations between aesthetic exemplification and moral exemplarity (starting from the paradigmatic *Don Quixote* by Cervantes); and finally, the tension between exemplarity and nonexemplarity inherent to modern literature, which questions existing models rather than proposing new ones.

Conceiving literature as a form of knowledge raises the questions of the relationship between literature and other forms of knowledge, and the uses to which it is put (Anheim and Lilti 2010; Sapiro 2023). Thus, unlike Naturalism, which uses medical knowledge without really questioning it, Surrealism makes literature an original means of exploring the unconscious (and the unconscious a source of literature). The degree of dependence or independence of the schemes of literary representation in relation to the existing frames of perception and analysis—whether they be mediatic, political, or scholarly—can thus constitute a principle for classifying works according to their capacity to renew the schemes of perceiving the world. This, in turn, invites "anthropological" readings of literary works (Bensa and Pouillon 2012). The question of how this knowledge is inscribed in the literary text also arises: the ironic distance with which Flaubert puts the commonplaces of his time in the mouths of such grotesque characters as the priest Bournisien and the free-thinking pharmacist Homais testifies to the capacity of literature to produce a relativizing effect on these discourses. Such irony reaches a peak in Flaubert's *Bouvard et Pécuchet,* which ridicules the title characters' quixotic ambition to embrace all the scientific knowledge of their time and narrates the saga of their delusions, and also of their disenchantments. Flaubert's posthumous *Le Dictionnaire des idées reçues* (*Dictionary of Received Ideas*) prolonged this satirical endeavor, which challenged the dominant worldview.

In this respect, literature can be considered a political discursive space. French critic Nelly Wolf (2005) proposes, for instance, an analysis of the novel as a site for the exploration of democracy and its limits. The "internal democracy" of the novel is observed at three levels. The first is that of fiction, through the questioning of the social contract whose implementation comes up against social hierarchies and mechanisms of exclusion. The second is that of diction, through the rapprochement of literary language with everyday language, but also through the representation of the gap between the legitimate language and the linguistic heterogeneity of popular dialects and languages, a gap introduced into literature by the Realists and Naturalists who kept the spoken language of the uneducated classes at a distance by marking the latter with quotation marks or italics, and probed by Céline who, in *Voyage au bout de la nuit* (*Journey to the End of the Night*), staged the conflictual character of this gap (on the gap between "dialects" and legitimate language, see Meizoz [2001]; Wolf [2019]). The third level is that of the discourse, through the fictitious staging of the battle of ideas by way of questioning and confronting different value systems—in a dialogical form, as in Diderot's *Jacques le fataliste* (*Jacques the Fatalist*), or in the form of the ideological novel studied by Susan Suleiman (1983). Situations of democratic transition provide a fertile site for observing the political uses of fiction and the models it proposes (on the Spanish case, see Bouju [2002]). One of the trends in contemporary literature is to dismantle the fictions produced by the media, the political sphere, and advertising, with the text's critical dimension prevailing over its representational and narrative activity (Brière and Gefen 2013).

To understand the role of literature in framing the perception of reality, it is therefore not enough to limit our focus to the

FIGURE 2. Literature between Representation and Symbolizing

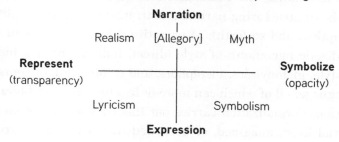

representations it contains. Literature oscillates in fact between representation and symbolization. On the side of representation, we tend to postulate the transparency of language and the primacy of the signified, and we make recourse to metonymy. On the side of symbolization, language is taken to be opaque, it signifies; here, metaphor reigns and attention is paid primarily to form. This first opposition must be combined with a second one (see Figure 2): the tension between narration and expression—which is not limited to the opposition between the novel and poetry, because it is found in the opposition between epic poetry and lyric poetry, for example (Sapiro 2011a; 2018a, 307).

This is why it is not sufficient to analyze the representations conveyed by a literary work in order to understand its specific character: the work of "formalization" (*mise en forme*)[3] is what transforms this raw material into a literary product identified as such.

The Work of Formalization

The literarization of material drawn from experience, from current events, from history, or from the imagination is carried out through the work of formalization (or formal processing), with the help of social and literary schemes for representing the world; of genres (the novel, poetry, theater); of subgenres (the picaresque novel, the Bildungsroman, and so on);[4] of formal models for structuring narrative (narrative order, temporality, description, and so forth); of narrative devices (omniscient or intradigetic narration); of style (direct, indirect, or free indirect style, metonymies, metaphors, and so on); and, of course, of language: all of which can more or less refer back to literary tradition. Formalization carries out this transubstantiation of material lived, imagined, or borrowed from external sources, and their amalgamation, whose principle escapes the author themself most of the time.

To analyze the process of "formalization," it is therefore necessary to bring to light the literary "ways of doing," that is to say, the "space of possibles" according to Bourdieu, or the "repertoire" of models (themes, styles, linguistic options) available at a given moment, according to Even-Zohar. The newcomers to the world of letters find an already formed space of possibles, which they must take into account and in relation to which they must define themselves. But how to reconstitute it?

From a methodological point of view, the relational approach made it possible to move away from essentialist hermeneutics in linguistics, with Roman Jakobson; in the history of ideas, with Ernst Cassirer and Michel Foucault; in the history of art, with Erwin Panofsky; and in literary studies, with the Russian formalists and later the structuralists (Todorov 2001). The structural analysis of narrative, which developed in France in the 1960s around the work of Roland Barthes, A. J. Greimas, and Claude Bremond, limited itself to an internal approach to texts. In the wake of Russian formalism, the theory of the "polysystem," conceived as a structured and hierarchical space of texts, offered more scope for the articulation between internal and external analyses (see chapter I). The concept of "repertoire," which designates the sets of models (themes, styles, linguistic options) available at a given moment in a given system, enables us to grasp the legitimate ways of making literature. The distinction between the "available" elements of the repertoire (those most often mobilized) and the "accessible" elements (those in the "stock" of models but seldom drawn upon) provides a heuristic for apprehending the mechanisms behind the evolution of literary forms. The systemic approach, however, is more functionalist than relational—unlike field theory, in which, as in structural linguistics, the meaning of the works emerges from the systems of differential gaps between and within them. It is the system of oppositions in which these works are placed that gives meaning to the options they embody. More than by common themes or devices, the works of the Nouveau Roman are united by their rejection of the main components of the Realist novel, namely, its characters, its plots, its messages. In the same way, the *nouveaux romanciers'* reference to Flaubert assumes its full significance if we relate it to their rejection of the Sartrean conception of engaged literature, then dominant in the intellectual field (Wolf 1995).

Unlike text-centered literary theories, field theory places further emphasis on the modus operandi, on creation as act (Bourdieu 1994). What makes some writers adopt certain models and not others? How are these models reinterpreted and readapted by them? To answer these questions, it is necessary to take into account the social characteristics of the writers, their positions in the field, and their trajectory. Indeed, the work of "formalization," which according to Bourdieu encloses all the history of the literary field, remains closely dependent on the point of view of the author (on the world and on the space of possibles) and bears its mark. Before examining the singularity of this point of view, I will look at the collective dynamics that mark the major developments in literary production, as well as at those that help, within a given configuration, to assign each person their place within the weakly regulated universe that is the world of letters.

Schools, Movements, Genres

As traditional objects of literary history (see, for instance, Schaeffer [1989]), the schools, movements, and genres that differentiate the world of letters also lend themselves to sociological analysis. Quantitative methods offer tools for grasping the diachronic variations (evolution of genres) and synchronic differences (comparative social recruitment by genre and school) therein.

Starting from the observation that the works forming the canon of literary studies represent less than one percent of novel production in the nineteenth century, Franco Moretti (1997, 2005) called upon his colleagues to shift their gaze from the "close reading" that predominates in their discipline to a "distant reading" by means of abstract models, the graphs of quantitative history, maps of geography and trees of evolutionary theory. In blending the approaches of literary historians with those of sociologists, who have resorted to quantitative methods, Moretti has opened up new perspectives in the field. The development of literary genres and subgenres at different times or in different cultures can thus be observed by way of bibliographic series: the rise of the novel follows the same curves of sudden evolution in Great Britain between 1720 and 1740, then in Japan between 1745 and 1765, in Italy between 1820 and 1840, in Spain from 1845 to the early 1860s, and finally in Nigeria between 1965 and 1980 (on the rise of the novel in Nigeria, see Griswold [2000]). In the same way, we see a succession of novelistic fashions: the epistolary novel, which triumphed in Great Britain between 1760 and 1790, was replaced, around 1800, by the gothic novel and then, from the 1820s, by the historical novel. In a similar vein, Ted Underwood (2019) combines genre and gender in a *longue durée* survey based on digital archives and computational methods.

His book, *Distant Horizons*, offers an overview of the fruitful uses of big data and computational methods for literary history.[5]

The prosopographic method enables us to link social properties with aesthetic choices (Ponton 1977; Charle 1979; Sapiro 1999/2014; Ducournau 2017; Leperlier 2019). This relation is not random. Thus, in the French literary field of the end of the nineteenth century, the psychological novelists were distinguished from the Naturalist novelists by their higher social origins, and by their higher educational capital: many of them had studied psychology at university, an education they then converted into their novelistic production (Ponton 1975).

The hierarchy of genres also corresponds to an unequal distribution of resources: the most socially endowed writers were those who were most successful in the lucrative genre of bourgeois theater, while poetry, placed at the pinnacle under the *ancien régime*, was marginalized with the rise of the book market, to the benefit of the novel, a previously popular and "feminine" genre, despised at the dominant pole of the literary field, but which nonetheless attracted, from the end of the nineteenth century onward, pretenders from the dominant fractions of the dominant class (Ponton 1977; Charle 1979).

The relation between social properties and aesthetic choices is not, however, direct: it is mediated by the conditions of access to the space of possibles, and by one's position in the literary field. It is therefore necessary to examine, first of all, the mediations between two spaces, the intellectual space of possibles and the distribution of forms of capital. These mediations, which are partly institutional, relate in some cases to the conditions of production and more generally to the structure of the social space.

One of the central mediations between the space of literary possibles and the resources of individuals is the educational system. It is partly the basis for the principle of reflexivity or self-referentiality in spaces of cultural production that, like the literary field, do not provide specialized training. Classical humanist culture, for example, was constitutive of the Western intellectual habitus for several centuries. Taught in France by the Jesuits, then by the secular secondary education system, this type of education was reserved, in the nineteenth century, for the sons of the bourgeoisie. Students entering *lycée* learned rhetoric, were taught figures of speech, and were trained to compose narratives in Latin and French. In rhetoric class, the *discours français* ("French discourse") was introduced, as well as the precepts of eloquence and the rules of all genres of writing. However, from the 1902 educational reform onward, humanistic culture began to compete with scientific culture, which was initially aimed at children from the middle classes. Representing, in many cases, the first generation that was not trained in the classical humanities, the Surrealists were in a way predisposed to make a break with the tradition of which they were not the custodians (Bandier 1999).

School is a mediator that is too often overlooked, a proper account of which would allow us to better define the space of possibles and what is thinkable for an intellectual generation, as well as their points of reference. One can, for example, wonder about the effects, within the French literary field, of the replacement of seventeenth-century authors—once the only writers taught—by eighteenth- and nineteenth-century writers in the *agrégation* curriculum at the turn of the twentieth century (Thiesse and Mathieu 1981).[6] However, to better grasp the logics of refraction within the field, it is necessary to take into account the original rivalry between *auctores* and *lectores*, between writers and professors (Boschetti 1985). This antagonism produced a situation in which access to the world of letters became conditioned, at least in France, by a show of distance from the school system. If Sartrean writing is strongly imbued with these scholastic models, it is only to better distance itself from them (Idt 1979).

Proust's juvenilia help us analyze the formation of his literary vocation and what it owes to his schooling (Kaës 2020).

The notions of "topicality" or "fashion" give a good account of what Durkheim calls social currents. They collude to dictate, at a given moment, the questions of the day, the literary agenda, the priorities, and the dominant taste—in short, what is called the *Zeitgeist*. In the intellectual sphere, "topicality" is constituted by publications in the general press and in specialized reviews, by reissues of older publications, publication of new books and translations, and by the reception of all of the above. The reissue of Cervantes's *Don Quixote* in the nineteenth century and the translations of Goethe and Byron, for example, were crucial to Flaubert's trajectory, just as the translations of Faulkner, Hemingway, and Dos Passos were to Sartre's. One way for an intellectual in training to distinguish themself from scholarly culture is to take an interest in little-known authors, as when the Surrealists discovered Lautréamont, or in authors belonging to lowbrow culture, like Marcel Allain and Paul Souvestre, authors of *Fantômas*. These sources then participate in a reconsideration of the literary orthodoxy of the moment.

Orthodoxy and Heterodoxy

Since Romanticism, the principle of originality has imposed itself as a way of affirming new entrants to the field. Significant evolutions are made by way of revolutions. The new currents or coteries innovate by updating models that were, in Even-Zohar's terms, merely "accessible" (rather than "available") in the literary repertoire of their time, or by importing them from another cultural space or another medium. Flaubert, for example, borrowed from Goethe his use of the impersonal narrator, and from medicine and painting his methods of observation and description.

This principle of originality often leads the new entrants to assert themselves by standing against the prevailing literary orthodoxy, embodied by the established writers occupying the dominant positions, who on their part struggle to maintain the existing balance of power. These struggles underlie the dynamics of change in the literary field (Bourdieu 1984a, 115/1993a, 73). Max Weber's sociology of religion provides tools for thinking about this opposition between orthodoxy and heterodoxy, between "priests" and "prophets": if priests are empowered by an institution (the Church), prophets base their power on their personal "charisma," the symbol of which is recognition by an "emotional community"—a sect (Bourdieu 1971b).

All the avant-garde movements, from the Romantics to the Surrealists (Bandier 1999) and the Situationists (Brun 2014) on through *Tel Quel* (Kauppi 1991/2013; Gobille 2005b), have asserted themselves against the orthodoxy of the literary establishment (on Italy, see Baldini [2023]). They often challenge the processes of differentiation within the intellectual field: the divisions of labor, specialization, gender, and so on. Operating as sects gathered around a prophetic figure, they do not, however, often manage themselves to escape from the process of social aging, which is accompanied by the routinization of their literary devices, the dilution of their message, and the institutionalization of some of their members, as Rémy Ponton (1973) has shown in his exemplary study of Parnassianism (see Box 6; and, for a study of Zutism based on the Weberian notion of "life conduct," see Denis Saint-Amand [2012]).

Literature and Identity

The method of collective biography opens up research prospects on the question of the relationship between literature and the construction of social identities. One of the cleavages that structures the space of possibles is indeed the tension between universalism and particularism. Imposed or claimed, identity has been a mode of affirmation for dominated writers in social space: local identity, religious identity, social identity, racial identity, gendered identity (Serry 2001). After Anne-Marie Thiesse's seminal work on regionalist novelists (Thiesse 1991), studies have been conducted on proletarian novelists (Aron 1995), Catholic writers (Serry 2004), Jewish writers (Clara Lévy [1998] detects a homology between a writer's relationship to Jewish identity and their relationship to writing; see also Zepp et al. [2020]; Wolf [2023]), the negritude movement (Malela 2008; see also Abiola Irele 2011), and "women's literature" (Naudier 2000, 2001).

However, the relationship between literature and identity is neither immediate nor automatic. Regionalism is a means of reconversion for writers of provincial origin who have not found their place in the Parisian world of letters. The conditions of access to this world remain very selective, socially speaking: white men, born in Paris or having emigrated there in their teens, from a privileged social background, and having a fairly advanced level of education have more chance of gaining recognition than women, people of color, people from the rural areas, children from the working classes, and those who do not have a high school education. Identity, which becomes relevant in the literary field from the beginning of the twentieth century, nevertheless opens up opportunities for professionalization in what economists call a publishing "niche" (found in publishing houses, collections, specialized journals), and in specific organizations. In the 1980s, the affirmation of "African literature" within French publishing houses and specialized collections such as Gallimard's "Continents noirs" followed a similar logic (Ducournau 2017). By the same token, the notion of *"beur"* literature[7] served to brand the literary production of French writers whose families came from North Africa, at a time when the *banlieues* (the peri-urban districts and neigh-

Box 6. The Routinization of Charisma:
The Case of Parnassus

In the preface to *Poèmes antiques* (1852), Leconte de Lisle, a poet until then relegated to the margins of the literary field as a mere imitator of the consecrated poets, defined the founding aesthetic principles of the Parnassian school, explicitly setting them against the poetic orthodoxy of the time: impersonality, political neutrality, study and experimentation, clearness of form. This heretical preface, which set out to radicalize the condition of marginality, was also prophetic in that it rallied a new generation around its watchwords and established a school. Erected as a prophet and a thought leader, Leconte de Lisle surrounded himself with a group of disciples forming a closed emotional community that he assembled weekly in his salon, with aspiring candidates being subjected to a rite of passage. In order to be maintained, such accumulated symbolic capital requires adequate methods of administration: enter the rationalization phase, which requires a reworking of the original message, of which only the prosodic precepts likely to be constituted as rules are retained—a process that contributes to their trivialization as the subversive tone is abandoned. Such a corpus of rules for versification reinforces the cohesion of the group while endowing it with instruments indispensable to the "concerted manipulation of their common symbolic capital" (Ponton 1973, 213). This symbolic capital earns them symbolic and temporal rewards in the long run: cooptation into the Académie Française, the Legion of Honor, official posts, critical positions in the mainstream press—all of which are marks of consecration that placed these writers in a dominant position within the field from the 1870s. This social ascent is reflected in the "making-worldly [*mondanisation*] of the Parnassian movement" (215): Leconte de Lisle's salon, formerly reserved for his peer group, opened up to newcomers and women, while his emancipated disciples launched their own salons. In the following decade, after the prophetic message had become highly routinized, it was the turn of Parnassian orthodoxy to be challenged by a new heresy, centered upon two figures: Verlaine, whose *Poètes maudits* (1883) reproduced Leconte de Lisle's techniques of rupture, and Mallarmé, who from 1885 onward gathered an anti-Parnassian circle at his house every Tuesday. The attitude of the elders toward their turbulent juniors oscillated between contempt and attempts at conciliation that resulted in a number of concessions, such as Sully-Prudhomme's ultimate acceptance of the hiatus in verse and of the nonalternation of masculine and feminine (a word ending with an "e") rhymes, as was the rule in French classical prosody. Thus, the crisis caused by the opposition to Parnassianism carried the Parnassians into a phase of prosodic casuistry that would conclude with the renunciation of its prophet after his death by most of his disciples (Ponton 1973).

borhoods where they grew up) were stigmatized, and when the antiracist political mobilizations were at a fever pitch (Kleppinger 2016; Harchi 2021).

Literature and the Nation

Of all the principles of identity, the one that has become most widely accepted is national identity: we speak of German, American, Italian, French writers, and so on, and of German, American, French, Italian literature, and so forth. As a result of the historical process of the nationalization of literature and, moreover, of literary history, this principle of identity prevails not only in the common representations of literature but also in scholarly conceptions. Now if, because of its medium, language, and the role it has played in the construction of national identities (Anderson 1983; Parkhurst Ferguson 1987; Corse 1997; Thiesse 1999/2022, 2020; Casanova 2011a/2011b), the link between literature and the nation corresponds to a social reality, the national literary canons have been formed by marginalizing and even excluding writers belonging to dominated social groups in this respect: immigrants, ethnic minorities, colonized or formerly colonized people—as postcolonial studies and subaltern studies have rightly pointed out (see below). Moreover, methodological nationalism tends to obscure the phenomena of cultural transfers and exchanges.

Until the end of the eighteenth century, classical education formed the common cultural foundation of the republic of letters in Europe, which communicated in Latin. This common ground disintegrated with the nationalization of culture in the nineteenth century, but, because of the place of classical studies in secondary education, it continued to nourish literate culture until the mid-twentieth century. For instance, British writers such as Oscar Wilde used classical Greek references to challenge the conservative Victorian conception of sexuality and to legitimize homosexuality (Evangelista 2009).

Beyond the common reference constituted by classical texts, national-language literatures were formed, initially, by the translation of works—in order to constitute a literary (and editorial) corpus in the national language, still in the process of codification—and by the importation of stylistic models, as shown by research carried out within the framework of polysystem theory.[8] Recognizing the original hybridity of national literatures enables us to relativize the idea that the phenomenon of *métissage*, or mixing between cultures, is specific to globalization.

The corpus of translated works was often the same from one language to another: these works, which came from the oldest literary languages (French, English, German, and Russian, in particular), thereby attained the status of universal masterpieces. A transnational canon was thus formed by the advent of national literatures, a canon that gradually replaced the classics of antiquity (Milo 1984) and that continued to expand, notably thanks to the creation of bodies of international consecration such as the Nobel Prize (which also adopted a national conception of literature [Sapiro 2020a]). By the end of the nineteenth century, the increasing circulation of literary works sparked debate and reflection on cosmopolitanism, challenging nationalist conceptions of culture (on the case of England, see Evangelista 2019).

The national framework also prevails in the critical approach to literary works, which are often inscribed in the cultural tradition of the country to which the writer belongs. This is because literary history, like history in general, is closely linked to the creation of national identities: the study of literature produced in the official language of a given country (American English, French, German, Italian) constitutes a discipline in its own right, distinct from that of literature published in other languages, which falls under either foreign language instruction or comparative literature. While comparative literature has promoted a more universalist (but often dehistoricized) conception of literature,[9] the study of cultural transfer originated mainly among specialists in foreign literatures, or in small countries such as Israel or Belgium, whose literature had not acquired full legitimacy, either because of its recency or because of its peripheral position in a linguistic area.

How to denationalize literary history? The best method is to historicize the categories of scholarly understanding. Thus, rather than hypostasize the opposition between nationalism and universalism, Pascale Casanova (1999) has adopted it as an object of sociohistorical research and as a prism through which to study the various strategies used by writers. This opposition thereby appears as constitutive of national literary fields: after the writers' initial investment in the construction of a national literature, a polarization emerges between those who remain enclosed in the national culture and those who look abroad. The "world republic of letters" was formed by the uprooting of national cultures, marking a major step in the process of the autonomization of literature. However, certain forms of literary nationalism could also be an instrument for emancipation, or for regaining independence in colonial contexts or under foreign occupation (as was the case in France during World War II), or for linguistic minorities (in Quebec or Galicia). We cannot therefore conclude that there is an intrinsic link between nationalism and heteronomy or between universalism and autonomy; this opposition must be considered in relation to the context in which it is inscribed, which leads us back to the study of the conditions of production.

The second contribution made by Pascale Casanova's sociohistorical approach is to resituate national literatures within a system of unequal exchanges. This inequality is a function of the literary capital of the national languages, which can be measured according to the number of works in this language that have been incorporated within a broader world heritage, the oldest literatures (French, English, German, Russian) having an advantage over the others.

The Postcolonial Perspective

The theoretical corpus of postcolonial studies has contributed to renewing the questions inherent to the sociology of literature. The problematic of identity based on national or social belonging is revisited from the perspective of migration, racialization, hybridity, and the position of the subaltern. These approaches follow in the wake of Edward Said's major work on the construction of the Orient in Western literary and artistic representation (Said 1978). Starting from the experience of eccentricity, postcolonial studies interrogate academic culture and the literary canon from the margins and the periphery—from repressed and "interstitial" spaces that challenge traditional forms of identification in terms of class, gender, and national belonging. Challenging the national construction of "imagined communities" (Anderson 1983), "these border and frontier conditions" (Bhabha 2012, 12) constitute places of enunciation for the subjects of postcolonial migration, of the cultural and political diaspora, and of the conditions of exile, slavery, and refugeehood. Homi Bhabha reads this "hybrid" experience of the "in-between" into Toni Morrison's *Beloved*, which depicts the condition of enslaved women through a story of infanticide, and Nadine Gordimer's *My Son's Story*, which describes the turmoil in South African ghetto homes under apartheid, through which the discomfort of mixed-race identity is revealed. For Bhabha, any reflection on "world literature," which has developed in connection with the process of globalization, must focus on "non-consensual terms of affiliation," through "the transnational histories of migrants, the colonized, or political refugees": "the center of such a study would be neither the 'sovereignty' of national cultures, nor the universalism of human culture, but a focus on those 'freak social and cultural displacements' that Morrison and Gordimer represent in their 'unhomely' fictions" (Bhabha 2012, 45).

However, such an approach is not sufficient to resolve the question posed by the deconstructivist Marxist feminist Gayatri Chakravorty Spivak in the title of her famous essay "Can the Subaltern Speak?" (1988). In that essay Spivak shows, through the example of Indian widow sacrifice rituals, the impossibility for subaltern women, torn between the patriarchal injunction (to immolate themselves after the death of their husbands) and the injunction of the English colonizer (to suppress this ritual considered barbaric), of expressing their own subjectivity. This leads her to question the representation of Third World subjects within Western discourse. In another article, analyzing a story by the Indian writer Mahasweta Devi Stanadayini (translated from Bengali into English by Spivak under the title *The Breast-Giver*), which the author conceived as a parable of postcolonial India through the figure of a wet nurse, Spivak tries to show how, beyond the parable, the story questions the presuppositions inherent in dominant feminist theories. Thus, the figure of the wet nurse calls into question the idea held by Anglo-American Marxist feminists that it is the sustenance provided to the woman by the man during the period of pregnancy that establishes the subordination of women in class society; by making childbirth a mode of access to free labor, the wet nurse also disturbs progressive or differentialist feminist conceptions that emphasize the reproductive (rather than "productive") function of the female body. Finally, through the analysis of the breast cancer that the wet nurse develops, Spivak shows the limits of a Lacanian reading of this work (Spivak 1987).

Postcolonial approaches have given rise to numerous publications on African and Caribbean literature, as well as on Indian writers. While most of them are limited to textual analyses, taking into account the sociopolitical context of colonialism and postcolonialism has also led to sociological readings of the works that constitute this corpus (see, for example, Miller [1998]; Moudileno [2000, 2006]; and Abiola Irele [2011]). Dominic Thomas (2006) demonstrates that the migratory experience takes a particular form in the works of African writers who received a French education under colonial rule, such as those by Camara Laye, Cheikh Hamidou Kane, Ousmane Socé, and Bernard Dadié, as well as in those of contemporary authors, such as Fatou Diome, Alain Mabanckou, or Daniel Biyaoula, the sojourn in France being the moment of confrontation between an imaginary that generates expectations and a reality that is often fraught with disenchantment. This prism enables Thomas to explore the bilateralism of Franco-African relations from the colonial period to the postcolonial era. In a similar vein, relying on archives and close readings, Elleke Bohmer (2015) has brought to light the interconnectedness of Indian intellectual migrants within British literary circles in *fin de siècle* Great Britain. And Subha Xavier (2016) has analyzed how "migrant texts" turn foreign cultures into literary commodities.

In her study on the literary system in Nigeria, based on interviews with authors, publishers, and readers, and on the study of some 500 novels, Wendy Griswold (2000) contrasts the themes and beliefs conveyed by this rich literary production with the living conditions in the country. Approaching the problematics of postcolonial studies by way of the sociology of literature has proved fruitful in renewing the questions specific to each of these two fields: on the one hand, the circulations of people and imaginary territories call into question the geographical boundaries of the literary field as well as the mechanisms of selection and consecration that are specific to it; on the other hand, the sociological analysis of trajectories and institutions makes it possible to resituate intellectual and aesthetic choices in a system of constraints and objective conditions that weigh on their orientation (on the trajectories of the francophone sub-Saharan writers, see Ducournau [2011, 2017]). In his work on Algerian literature, Tristan Leperlier (2019) speaks of a bilingual and transnational literary field, which is positioned at the periphery of the French-speaking world (the center of which is Paris) and the Arab-speaking one (whose publishing centers are in Cairo and Lebanon).

Aesthetic Singularity as Sociological Object of Study

While the collective dimension, especially identity (nation, class, ethnicity, gender), is often emphasized in approaches to literatures located at the periphery of the world republic of letters and to the least legitimated genres (proletarian literature, North African or *"beur"* literature, women's literature, and so on), studies devoted to well-known writers insist on the singularity of those writers, which is considered irreducible to social parameters. The sociology of literature is often identified with the collective dimension. However, far from a sociological reductionism that would tend to dissolve the original character of the works into the "social," the sociology of literary works aims at understanding their true originality.

The Biographical Approach to Literature

The biographical approach, which traditionally prevails in the external analyses of the most legitimated works and which constitutes a rather lucrative editorial genre, reinforces the paradigm of singularity (Heinich 2005), which governs the artistic spheres. It found its most successful philosophical expression with the idea of the creative project that Sartre (1988a) develops in his biography of Flaubert. In accordance with the ultra-individualist and ultra-subjectivist ideology that prevails in the literary field, Sartre anchors the creative project solely in the biography of the creator. Yet, any individual step is inscribed in a space of possibles that presents itself to the writer, and in the social conditions of its materialization, which are inflected by interactions with one's entourage, peers, editors, and critics.

Therefore, the sociological analysis of the production of works must, per Bourdieu, study the encounter between habitus and field, the internalization of the space of possibles being one of the conditions of possibility for knowing the rules of the game and participating in its self-reflexivity—the reference the field makes to its own history—both of which characterize the field's relative autonomy. What seems obvious at first becomes less so when we set out to implement this approach. Indeed, nothing is less simple than to study the way in which a space of possibles was or has been perceived and internalized by cultural producers. How do they perceive the space of positions and the space of possibles at a given moment? In relation to which positions, to which position-takings, do they define themselves? What are the options available to them according to the types of capital they hold? These are the questions that must guide research on a methodological level.

It is by their trajectories that individuals distinguish themselves. This notion of trajectory, which designates the series of positions successively occupied by the same individual or group in a social space in transformation, aims to break with the "biographical illusion" (Bourdieu 1986/2017), a teleological conception of life as a linear, coherent, directional path, the unitary expression of an intention or an original project. Works of literature sometimes enclose traces of the author's trajectory: for instance, Jules Romains's *Les Hommes de bonne volonté* (*Men of Good Will*), published in twenty-seven volumes between 1932 and 1946, is strewn with the metaphors of upward mobility that characterize his itinerary, but the "passion to succeed" has undergone a process of euphemization imposed by the ethic of disinterestedness that prevails in the world of letters (Memmi 1998).

However, even when one has, as for Flaubert or Sartre, reliable sources concerning what they read, and even if traces of that reading can be found in an explicit or implicit manner in their writing—as with references to Shakespeare and Cervantes in the works of Flaubert—that is ultimately not enough to account for the work of transubstantiation performed by the act of creation, which remains a "black box." Moreover, the space of possibles is not internalized in complete isolation. It is necessary to take into account all the reactions, feedback, and sanctions that orient the choices of newcomers and lead them to readjust their strategy. After having read his *Tentation de Saint-Antoine* (*The Temptation of Saint Anthony*) all night to his friends Bouilhet and Du Camp, Flaubert was told that it should be thrown in the garbage. From this came the project of *Madame Bovary*, his friends having suggested to him that, to counterbalance his romantic disposition, he should take on a more banal and contemporary subject, as Balzac had done in *Le Cousin Pons* or *La Cousine Bette*.

In the same spirit, Sergio Miceli (2007) reconstructed the system of family, cultural, and social constraints in which the young Borges was caught and the dispositions that led him to reconvert the disappointed hopes of the declining *criollo* circles into a literary vocation that propelled him to the head of the Argentine avant-garde.

Asking how Gabriel García Márquez produced a novel that

would become a classic, Álvaro Santana-Acuña (2020) identifies a set of relevant sociohistorical factors. Márquez's imagination was first fed by his personal experience (especially his youth) and by his literary networks in Colombia. Despite his peripheral geographic origins and low social origins, Márquez was able to acquire the skills (through his reading of Latin American and international writers such as Faulkner and Hemingway, as well as through his professional experience as a journalist) and the social capital that allowed him to become recognized as a Colombian writer. Geographic mobility enabled him to enter a large Latin American intellectual network, which gave him access to prestigious periodicals and ensured him support—not only moral, social, and financial, but also collaborative—for his literary projects. But none of these factors would have been as powerful without a specific conjuncture, called the "Latin American boom," a notion that needs to be deconstructed in order to reconstruct more accurately the sociohistorical conditions that enabled this label to acquire symbolic value on the international book market, at a time when other trends, such as Social Realism or the Nouveau Roman, were declining. This label did not emerge spontaneously but was promoted by the intellectual network Márquez belonged to (and which included already famous authors such as Fuentes, Vargas Llosa, and Cortazar); he modified *One Hundred Years of Solitude* while writing it to better fit the label. He erased, for instance, overly specific references to Colombia so that the story could be said to have taken place anywhere in rural Latin America, and he adopted a baroque style that he had rejected in his previous work. The "Latin American boom" was marketed by gatekeepers, especially publishers in Argentina and Spain, and by Spanish literary agent Carmen Balcells, who promoted Latin American authors on the international market.

Symbolic Revolutions

The concept of "symbolic revolution," coined by Bourdieu, refers to the redefinition of the space of possibles by innovative works. Baudelaire, whom Bourdieu calls a nomothete, in that he established practices freed from submission to external powers and from the publishing marketplace (he opted for a small avantgarde publisher, Poulet-Malassis), from criticism (which he practiced himself), and from access to recognition (his candidacy for the Académie Française was a provocation), overcame, in his poetry, the opposition between Romantic lyricism and Parnassian objectivism to reach a "realist formalism," of which the work that Flaubert carried out on composition and the French language constituted an equivalent (Bourdieu 1992, 157–58/1996, 107–8; for an application of the concept of "realist formalism" to the work of Olivier Cadiot, see Boschetti [2003]).

This redefinition, which modifies the principles of perception and the practices within the field, is an objective fact, which can be measured by the scandal that these works caused at the time of their first publication. This can be seen, for example, in the case of Flaubert's use of free indirect speech in *Madame Bovary*, which opened the way to the modern novel. Unlike their peers, who simply replicated established models, these cultural producers transformed the space of possibles. But such innovations are not made *ex nihilo*. It is often by the importation of models from another field, as Thomas Kuhn suggests in the case of scientific revolutions, or by the synthesis between previously opposing options that they take place. Thus, the refusal of representation led Beckett to transpose to literature the work of abstraction being carried out at the same time in painting (Casanova 1997).

Poetry, in which the formal dimension is more prevalent and the rules of composition more constraining, constitutes a privileged site for observing symbolic revolutions. The originality of the young Mallarmé does not lie in his choice of material, borrowed from post-Romanticism, or in the formal schemes he adopts, but in the radical treatment he applies to them by pushing to the extreme the haunting of the Ideal and the pure and disinterested gesture that the poet sketches in its direction, as well as in the contrasts between this Parnassian purity of the ideal and the Baudelairian horror of reality (Durand 2008). These contrasts are expressed, against a background of trivial representations, in the language of abjection and disgust that breaks with the ethereal formulas of the quest for "The Azure."

Refusing the alternative between tradition and modernity, Guillaume Apollinaire transcended both by integrating the neo-Symbolist and decadent heritages, and creating a new, experimental aesthetic of the discontinuous, in tune with the techniques of collage and montage in the visual arts, painting, and cinema. His dialogue with modern painters helped to legitimize their anti-Naturalist aesthetic, all of them finding common cause in the slogan of "simultaneity," around which the competition within the avant-garde was tightening. His poem-conversations and his "calligrams" are, like collages, nonfigurative painting, and the ready-made, an expression of the increasing reflexivity of artistic activity, questioning the relationship between art and the real world and the principles for designating an object as a work of art (Boschetti 2001).

These works link aesthetic choices to the dispositions of the author under study. Apollinaire's status as an emigrant, Beckett's Irish origins, Kafka's background as a member of the German Jewish minority in Prague (Casanova 2011c/2015a; see Box 7), are articulated together with these authors' social properties and their singular trajectories to explain their choices within a particular space of possibles.

The renewal of the space of literary possibles is achieved through the deployment of writing strategies. For instance,

Box 7. Kafka, Ethnologist of Domination

Pascale Casanova analyzes Kafka's choices among the options available to his generation of German-speaking Jewish intellectuals in Prague, who broke with the assimilationism of their fathers and sought a national identity—an identity that they believed they had discovered in the traditions and customs of the Jewish communities of Eastern Europe at a time when these communities were in the process of liberating themselves. While most of these intellectuals opted for Zionism, Kafka found in the burgeoning Yiddish theater a truly national and popular art. As an ethnologist of the Jewish people, he explores in his works, in a cryptic manner, the symbolic violence that underlies assimilation, which was being denounced at the same time by his Zionist friends. He approaches this from various perspectives: as impasse, as betrayal, as loss, as guilt, as individual and collective tragedy, and so on. "In the stories and novels, particularly *The Trial,* the desire for assimilation is embodied in characters who obey a mandatory—though not explicitly stated—law which forces them to submit to the rules of a society that despises and humiliates them, despite the fact that no physical violence compels them to do so and they are not clearly aware of the law in question. It follows that the hidden centre of Kafka's oeuvre is a (highly critical) reflection on domination" (Casanova 2011, 359; 2015, 284).

Carlo Emilio Gadda and Claude Simon's engaged use of form differentiated itself from both Sartre's committed literature and art for art's sake (Benaglia 2020). This leads us to the notion of strategy.

Writing Strategies and Authorial Strategies

If many decisions in the act of writing escape intentionality—which cannot be reconstituted on the sole basis of an internal textual analysis, requiring sources that are not always available, such as drafts, notes, and correspondence used in the genetic study of manuscripts—the notion of strategy, theorized by Bourdieu, is no less useful in the sociology of literature. Unlike abstract theories about rational actors, strategies only make sense in relation to dispositions (habitus) and to a system of constraints. However, unlike structuralism, which makes social agents the simple bearers of structures, the notion of strategy was aimed at restoring a margin of maneuverability to individuals. It is thus a heuristic concept for the empirical study of an agent's behaviors. And it works by questioning the agents' ability to devise, according to their dispositions, behaviors well adjusted to given situations; the degree of consciousness that presided over their chosen behaviors; and the types of rationality to which these behaviors belong.

Literary history grants us a rich empirical terrain for studying social strategies. One should, in this framework, distinguish "writing strategies"—in the sense of the intentionality of the act of writing—from "authorial strategies." These strategies are not reducible to interest or profit-oriented rationality. Writing strategies refer to the work of anticipation and to the objectives to which that work is more or less subordinated (which can be redefined as the work progresses). Strategies are more or less conscious: if the processes of subverting conventions are often at least partly due to conscious choices—except in the limit case that, in art history, we denote for this reason with the adjective "naïve"— we nevertheless cannot entirely identify semantic intension with psychological intention. On the one hand, the process of writing goes far beyond the conscious strategy of the author. On the other, the meaning of the work is inseparable from the context of its reception, which largely escapes the author (see chapter IV). This is why the notion of "choice," which can be substituted for that of strategy, does not solve the problem of the nonthetical action, and why it must be related to the concept of habitus, especially as the choices, the strategies, are themselves conditioned by the dispositions of the individual.

The notion of strategy is also a heuristic for studying the spheres of creation, where individuals must impose themselves and make a name for themselves in order to exist. The author's strategies aim at accumulating symbolic capital in order to attain consecration. These strategies are more or less oriented toward symbolic recognition (by peers and authorities specific to the literary field) or worldly (*temporel*) recognition (literature as a means of accessing social success, through the conversion of notoriety into economic, social, and/or sometimes political capital). The relationship between, on the one hand, the strategies implemented in the work of writing and the way in which they submit to the rules of the game or subvert them and, on the other hand, the social strategy of the author in search of recognition opens up a vast field of research to the sociology of literature: To what extent are the strategies of writing adjusted or subordinated to this second objective (recognition)? To what extent are they appropriate and efficient? To what extent does this efficiency depend on the knowledge of the rules of the game? And what about the so-called "naïve" creators, that is to say, those who are not strategic and rather ignorant of the rules?

Postures and Authorial Scenarios

The writer's life and work are the object of staging and worship, giving rise to "authorial strategies." According to José-Luis Diaz (2007, 257), Romanticism conducted a revolution by putting the writer "in the center of the stage, not only as author of the work, but also as existential subject and transcendental principle." Anxious to distinguish itself from bourgeois mores, the aristocratic aesthetic attitude took, as a form of "self-presentation" (Goffman) and bodily hexis, the form of dandyism, embodied notably by Baudelaire and Wilde. This found its extension in the bohemian lifestyle (Seigel 1986). Anticonformism would continue, in the twentieth century, to characterize the way of life of many writers and artists under various forms.

But "posture" is not limited to self-presentation and lifestyle. Alain Viala (1988; 1993, 216) defines it as the "manner of occupying a position," linking it to "literary strategy." Jérôme Meizoz (2007) extends it to the dimension of rhetoric, which José-Luis Diaz (2007) for his part refers to as "authorial scenarios [*scénarios auctoriaux*]." In the Romantic period, the preface was their privileged locus of enunciation, but they are often found scattered throughout the works themselves. Jean-Jacques Rousseau thus made elective poverty a mark of virtue and purity, inaugurating a form of economic independence in comparison to writers who were stipendiaries of the state, living on offices and pensions (Meizoz 2003). Laying claim to the author of *Confessions*, Henry Poulaille, C. F. Ramuz, and Jean Giono would assert their own posture of "authenticity" (on Ramuz, see Meizoz [1997]). The fact of being a doctor, which set him apart from, even *outside* of, the literary world, did much to confer upon Louis-Ferdinand Céline his *auctoritas* as a writer (Roussin 2005).

Memoir is the traditional genre of self-presentation for a public figure looking to provide their testimony of an era. This genre, largely abandoned by writers in the twentieth century in favor of autobiography, was nevertheless revisited by certain authors, such as Malraux and Beauvoir (Jeannelle 2008).

In the twentieth century, the press became one of the venues in which the figure of the author was performed. The genre of the literary interview developed at the end of the nineteenth century, with Jules Huret's survey on "literary evolution"; it became institutionalized in the interwar period with Frédéric Lefèvre's column "Une heure avec . . ." in *Les Nouvelles littéraires*. If the diversification of media and the cult of the writer's personality have favored the proliferation of sites of enunciation for the "authorial" posture, writers such as Christine Angot (Fassin 2001) and Michel Houellebecq have made the staging of the self the main theme of their work. These "authorial strategies" must be distinguished from the "writing strategies" of the main authors associated with the genre of autofiction, such as Annie Ernaux (who rejects the term, preferring that of autosociobiography) or Camille Laurens, whose work is characterized by the shaping of lived experience within the framework of an approach that oscillates between introspection and testimony (Sapiro 2013a, 2013b; on Ernaux, see Thumerel [2004]).

Representation, exemplarity, construction of collective identities, symbolic revolutions, postures and self-staging are so many phenomena that raise, beyond the sociology of works, the question of the conditions of their reception, from success to scandal.

IV

The Sociology of Reception

A literary work's meaning stems in large part from readers' own interpretations and appropriations of the text and therefore is not reducible to the author's intent. These readings are determined by the possibilities opened up by the text and by a whole system of mediations, ranging from the editing of the text to the work's adaptations and critical reception. While literary texts (which are more or less ambiguous or polysemous) offer room for these interpretations (Eco 1989), sometimes the interpretations go so far as to get the texts to say things they don't actually say. The circulation of literary texts across space and time, and beyond the context of their production (Bourdieu 2002a/1999b), facilitates these attempts at annexation. The sociology of reception consists in analyzing these mediations and uses of literature.

The sociological perspective thus broadens the approach to reception developed by Hans Robert Jauss and the Constance School, which is limited to the study of texts. Reacting against ahistorical hermeneutic criticism, positivist literary history, and Marxist reflection theory, Jauss (1982) argues in favor of an antipositivist literary history that conceptualizes reception as the history of effects produced by works of literature. The key concept in this approach is the "horizon of expectations," which Jauss borrows from Husserl, Mannheim, and Popper, and applies to literary phenomena. The works of literature that leave a mark on literary history are those that at the time of publication break with readers' horizon of expectations, which is informed by a set of previously published texts from the same genre.

Yet the reader imagined by Jauss is an abstract one, whose horizon of expectations can only be reconstructed through the study of texts. Instead, sociology is interested in real readers. Moreover, just like production, reception is a process mediated by the material or intellectual modalities for the presentation of literary works, the reactions elicited among literary critics and other institutions, and the modes of appropriation by different reading publics, depending on their social characteristics. Before delving into the question of reading and reading publics, we'll begin by looking at the authorities that mediate the process of reception.

Mediating Authorities

The reception of a literary text is inextricably linked to its public appraisal. The sociology of literature takes as its object of study the ways texts are hierarchized within the space of reception, through the processes of selection, classification, and ranking that critics, the press, and authorities of distribution and consecration perform; all of which is reflected in the critical success of the texts, sales figures, inclusion on bestseller lists, literary prizes, institutional consecration, and so on. These forms of recognition may stand in contradiction to one another. In France, since the mid-nineteenth century, commercial success has rarely been compatible with recognition from one's peers, mainstream success being suspected to be the fruit of compromise, or even compromising behavior—that is to say, submission to heteronomous forces.

Stages and Stakes of Reception

Although analytically useful, the distinction between the conditions of production and reception should not mask the active intervention of cultural intermediaries in framing the reception of works of art. Roger Chartier (1988) distinguishes two processes: the *mise en texte* (textualization), which refers to the author's writing strategies in order to frame the interpretation of their work, and the *mise en livre* (transforming a text into a book), which designates all the editors' interventions in the publishing process (see also Chartier 1994, 1996; Mackenzie 1999).

Reception is therefore first mediated by the modes of publication and distribution: the paratext (the dedication page, preface, afterword, back cover [Genette 1997]), medium (press, article in a specialized journal, brochure, book), and place and environment in the medium (the exact location of an article on the newspaper's page or the inclusion of a book in a collection). Publishers play an important role in the process by inscribing the work in an editorial collection, curating its presentation in the catalog, writing the back cover text, and creating the packaging, namely, the cover, the book jacket, and the promotional wrap-around band, or *bandeau*. The cover allows the informed reader to situate the book within a genre and category at a glance: the "iconographic" covers in loud colors typical of bestsellers and books intended for mass-market distribution, for instance, in "big box" stores, contrast sharply with the sober "typographic" covers typical of upmarket literature, at least in France (Rigot 1993). The work of a publisher continues even after book production: running publicity through brochures and websites, choosing a distributor, drafting blurbs for booksellers, sending advance review copies to the press, sending flyers to retailers and bookstores, setting up displays at points of sale, seeking media coverage or placing an advertisement, organizing public readings, lectures, and promotion tours in the country and abroad, and so on.

The paratext constitutes another essential mediation. Asking an established writer to preface a text by a debut author or a translated author used to be a classic way of legitimizing a book in upmarket literary publishing. Pierre Drieu La Rochelle and André Malraux, for instance, were each asked by their publisher, Gallimard, to write a preface for the French translations of Hemingway's *A Farewell to Arms* (1932) and Faulkner's *Sanctuary* (1933), respectively. Malraux defined *Sanctuary* as "the intrusion of Greek tragedy in the crime novel," thus presenting this work at once as innovative through the mixture of apparently incompatible genres, and as universal thanks to its reference to the classical tradition (Sapiro 2016b). As this example shows, the paratext also contributes to categorizing the text according to genre (here crime fiction and tragedy), literary tradition (here Greek), schools, movements, trends (for instance, Romanticism, Realism, Surrealism, Magical Realism). A preface can also be a means of annexation: for example, in his preface to Nathalie Sarraute's *Portrait d'un inconnu* (*Portrait of a Man Unknown*), originally published in 1948, Sartre claimed her work for existentialist literature, a decade before she became a prominent figure of the Nouveau Roman. Today, blurbs on the back cover tend to replace prefaces, as they can be read quickly in the bookstore or online, and can thus help to distinguish products in a conjuncture of overproduction.

Book series or imprints in a conglomerate also structure production and distribution by categorizing them. Book series are organized around genres (novel, poetry, theater), distinguishing genre literature such as crime novels or science fiction. In

France, since the 1930s, "foreign literature" (translated works) is usually kept separate from "French literature" (which tends to include francophone authors). Specific series are sometimes devoted to a geographic or cultural area. In the 1950s, for instance, Gallimard launched, alongside its foreign literature series "Du monde entier," three collections: "Connaissance de l'Orient" for works from East Asia (Japan, China, and India), "La Croix du Sud" for Latin American authors, and "Littératures soviétiques" for contemporary Russian writers (Sapiro 2015a). The catalog of Actes Sud, which has specialized in foreign literature since its establishment in 1979, is organized in series based on linguistic areas, in accordance with the editors' specialization. "Identity," whether national, gendered, or "racial," is a means for making dominated writers visible and for accumulating symbolic capital collectively: for instance, some series focus on authors from Africa and the Caribbean, such as CARAF books at University of Virginia Press.

Thus, the media (newspapers, literary magazines, brochures, books) and the surroundings (for example, the other texts on the newspaper page or in the journal, the other titles in a series or in book club subscriptions) participate in the reception process as they frame the perception of the text and its categorization. For instance, under the German occupation in France, during World War II, the communist writer Claude Morgan warned his peers in the underground journal *Les Lettres françaises* not to publish in the legal press, which was under Nazi control. He gave the example of a harmless article by Colette on Burgundy that appeared in the collaborationist news weekly *La Gerbe* beside a text by the mayor of Freiburg am Brisgau, Dr. Reimer, titled "A Land between Rhine and Rhone," which described Burgundy as a region of great interest for Germans and a strategic place for Franco-German collaboration. This example demonstrated, according to Morgan, how any innocent literary contribution to the legal press could be diverted to legitimize Nazi propaganda (Sapiro 2014, 46).

After publication, reception is mediated by interpretations and strategies of annexation of the work by a network of agents (individuals or institutions), including professionals (critics, peers) and nonprofessionals, who belong to the literary or intellectual fields (journals, juries, academies) or to other fields, such as the political, legal, medical, or psychoanalytical fields, whether organizations (censorship boards, associations, morality leagues) or private initiatives (such as reading clubs). These appropriations can be contradictory: Louis-Ferdinand Céline's *Voyage au bout de la nuit (Journey to the End of the Night)*, originally published in 1932, was acclaimed on the political right as well as the left. Cases of multiple appropriations are particularly interesting, since, through labeling and attempts to annex the work, they reveal the issues at stake in the field of reception. Such ideological struggles can condition the variable reception of an author over time, as Paul Nizan's "posthumous career" illustrates: a communist writer who died in 1939 in the war, accused of being a traitor by the Communist Party from which he resigned following the Molotov-Ribbentrop Pact, Nizan was "rehabilitated" in 1960 when the leftist publisher Maspero reissued his book *Aden Arabie* with a preface by his former prep school [*khagne*] classmate, Jean-Paul Sartre, who, on the eve of May 1968, turned him into a figurehead for rebellious youth (Pudal 1994).

Beyond political organizations, professional organizations and literary authorities can enact a form of censorship at once linguistic, ideological, and racial, which the conflicts surrounding a given book unveil. The history of the Prix Goncourt provides examples of this. In 1920, the conservative members of the jury tried to push back against the choice made by other jury members to award the prize to René Maran, the author of *Ba-*

touala, because he had criticized the colonial administration and above all because he was Black (how could a Black author represent French literature? they asked). In the case of *Voyage au bout de la nuit* the jurors who reproached Céline for transgressing the rules of linguistic propriety won out over his supporters (Sapiro 2014, 254–60/1999, 330).

Other forms of censorship are also implemented by authorities responsible for distribution, from large publishing conglomerates that engage in economic censorship to public libraries whose selections tend to reflect their "middle" or in-between position in the sociocultural space—somewhere between the cutting-edge taste of the fractions endowed with the most cultural capital, considered elitist, and that of underprivileged classes, relegated to vulgarity—rather than their pedagogical function (on Parisian public libraries, see Rabot 2015). The American Library Association's Office for Intellectual Freedom (OIF) compiles a list of the most banned and challenged books in libraries and schools (in the large majority of cases at the initiative of conservative organizations or parent interest groups). The motives range from an objection to depictions of violence, sexuality, profanity, and/or anti-patriotism, to racism, and they vary over time (though some recur). This list included, for the period 2010–19, two modern classics: J. D. Salinger's *The Catcher in the Rye* and Toni Morrison's *Beloved*.[1]

Reception is a process that extends beyond the framework of a work's production in a particular time and space (for instance, new publications, translations), and that modifies the environment, at times leading to revaluations, as demonstrated by the example of Paul Nizan. The change in the context of reception may alter the meaning attributed to a work and its appraisal. Certain works that provoked a scandal in the past, such as Flaubert's *Madame Bovary* or Baudelaire's *Les Fleurs du mal*, have become classics. The sentence against Baudelaire was even revised in 1949, almost one century after the 1857 trial, by a legal procedure created for his case. This example shows once again that reception is a process mediated by agents, be they individuals or institutions. The reversal of the conviction is an extreme case that is revelatory of the process of canonization.

The educational system plays a central role in this process of canonization, or "classicization" (Viala 1993), through scholarship devoted to authors (PhD dissertations, articles, books) and through course syllabi. Publishing houses also participate in this process, by reissuing the work of dead authors and publishing series devoted to the complete (or selected) works of an author, such as Gallimard's *"Bibliothèque de la Pléiade"* (Gleize and Roussin 2009), or anthologies (Fraisse 1997; on the case of Colette, see André [2000]).

Since references to the history of the field are essential to cementing its relative autonomy, the rediscovery of writers from the past by an author or a group of writers often serves the latter's own legitimization and can be used to contest the established definition of literature. The Surrealists resurrected Lautréamont, and the Nouveau Roman appropriated Flaubert, who had been criticized by Sartre for not having engaged during the Paris Commune. In his genealogy of the figure of the committed responsible writer, Sartre included Voltaire and Zola. Reference to foreign authors may also serve purposes of self-legitimization (see below).

Quarrels, controversies, and polemics reveal the space of possibles made tangible in the literary works themselves and in the judgments passed on them by peers and critics (for instance, the "bad masters quarrel" during the German occupation [Sapiro 1999, 161–202/2014, 122–45]). Literary trials count among the most heuristic sites for reconstructing the "horizon of expectations" and its limits.

Literary Trials

Political regimes that adopt the principle of freedom of expression shift their ideological and moral control from prepublication (prior censorship) to postpublication, that is, from the stage of production (preceding publication) to the stage of reception. It has been shown that censors often act as literary critics (McDonald 2009). Like prior censorship, legal proceedings brought against works of literature constitute a good indicator of the existing boundaries of what can be said or represented in a given sociohistorical configuration, but also of their liability across time and space, as the examples of Flaubert's *Madame Bovary* or Baudelaire's *Les Fleurs du mal*, both taken to court in 1857, illustrate.

Among the reasons for the scandal caused by *Madame Bovary* was the disappearance of the author's moral person behind his characters (the impersonal narrator) and his use of a new literary device, free indirect speech, two devices that were to become typical of the modern novel, but that led to misunderstanding at that time. The prosecutor blamed Flaubert for not judging his main character, Emma, as the classical norm imposed. He also accused him of praising adultery, drawing from the passages where the narrator embraced Emma's point of view, using free indirect speech (Jauss 1982; LaCapra 1982; Leclerc 1991; Sapiro 2011b). More recently, in France, Nicolas Jones-Gorlin's *Rose Bonbon* (2002), a novel written in the first person that depicts a pedophile, was criticized on similar grounds, echoing the debates around *Lolita* (1955) by Nabokov (on the latter, see Ladenson [2007]). The scandals spurred by these books are simultaneously aesthetic and moral, because by voicing an illegitimate point of view, the texts break taboos held by what Émile Durkheim called the "collective consciousness."

When writers are on trial, the interpretation of their works becomes the subject of debate (LaCapra 1982; Leclerc 1991; Ladenson 2007; Sapiro 2007c, 2011b). These debates exploit the ambiguity of literary texts that use fiction, codes, allusions, metaphors, and different temporal settings to circumvent bans. Whereas the prosecutor attempts to reveal an author's presumed ideological intentions, the defense often adopts a strategy of denial that aims to confine the text strictly to the literary sphere (not without bad-faith arguments). Literary forms and genres are often brought up in these debates. Tried in 1890 for insults made against the army and for crimes against public decency and morality, Lucien Descaves saw his *Sous-Offs* defined as "vile libel" by the assistant public prosecutor when his defending attorney tried to explain the difference between a novel and a lampoon. While the author's intentions (and/or that of the publisher when the author is dead) refer to their own subjective responsibility, their objective responsibility, from the standpoint of law, lies in the conditions of publication (whether it is printed in a book or newspaper, if the print runs are small or large), which provide information about the reading public the publication might reach; and it is also seen in the presumed effects of the text on its readership, according to commonsense theories of reception (Sapiro 2011b, 2016d). For instance, Judge Woolsey, who in 1933 examined the case of Joyce's *Ulysses*, which was prosecuted for obscenity in the United States, argued that "whilst in many places the effect of *Ulysses* on the reader undoubtedly is somewhat emetic, nowhere does it tend to be an aphrodisiac" (Segall 1993). To successfully carry out this work of interpretation, judges and lawyers often look to the prosecuted book's critical reception.

Critical Reception

Literary criticism constitutes one of the main mediations in the process of the reception and valorization of works of literature at the pole of upmarket literature, in contrast to commercial genres. Its existence signals a certain degree of institutionalization of literary activity, and its relative autonomy. This mediation is a major source for studies on the reception of literary works, given that literary criticism lends itself easily to the interpretive tradition of the human sciences (although it can also be explored with lexicometrical and digital methods). Joseph Jurt's pioneering study on the critical reception of the work of Georges Bernanos combined qualitative and quantitative analysis: articles on Bernanos's writings were categorized depending on whether the reviews were positive or negative and according to the style of the periodical, its frequency of publication, its place of publication, and its political orientation (Jurt 1980). Annie Ernaux's works provide a particularly interesting case study for analyzing how aesthetic and social judgments, as well as issues related to gender, are intertwined in contemporary French literary criticism (Charpentier 1994).

The criteria for assessing literary works depend on the critic's position within the literary field. Discourses on literature indeed vary according to two main factors that structure the literary field. The first, which pits "the dominants" against "the dominated," distinguishes orthodox conceptions of literature from heterodox or heretical ones. The more dominant the position held by a critic, the more they will adopt a euphemized and depoliticized discourse—at least in their form and style—following the rules of decorum of intellectual debate. Conversely, the more dominated the position held by the critic, the more politicized their discourse and the more they denounce the dominant viewpoint's conformism and conventionality.

The second factor, which pits autonomy against heteronomy, opposes two ideal-typical conceptions of literature and critical discourses: on the one hand, those that tend to focus on content (for instance, story, plot, and moral values) and, on the other hand, those that prioritize form (narrative and poetic structure) and style, proof of the growing logic of autonomization and reflexivity within the fields of cultural production.

The intersection of these two axes—dominant/dominated and autonomy/heteronomy—creates four quadrants, representing four ideal types (in Max Weber's sense) of discourses on literature. The dominant discourse at the heteronomous pole of the field takes the form of moral judgment: literature is regarded as a means to maintain the social and moral order, whereas the dominated discourse at this pole is based more on political or social criteria. At the dominant autonomous pole, it is aesthetic judgment that holds sway, whereas at the avant-garde, where routinization is condemned as a form of orthodoxy, the renewal of literary forms is understood to be a means of social subversion (see Figure 3).

FIGURE 3. Ideal Types of Critical Discourses

	DOMINANT	
	Orthodoxy	
	Academic*	
	Aesthetic	**Moral**	
AUTONOMY			
Form, style,			HETERONOMY
formalization	**Critical**	**Political**	*Content*
	DOMINATED	
	Heterodoxy	
	Politicized	

*"Academic" here doesn't mean "scholarly," but rather "conventional, official, institutional, dominant."

Without going so far as to deny any well-argued grounds for the judgment exercised by critics, that judgment is based not solely on criteria intrinsic to the work, but also on external criteria, such as the writer's symbolic capital (if they are not a debut author), the publisher's reputation (which carries more weight for debut authors), and the judgments passed by previous critics. These factors explain the phenomenon of the concentration of criticism on a small number of titles. It has been shown that 50 percent of criticism published over the course of the year 1978 concerning Dutch literary production concentrated on 10 percent of the titles that came out that year (half of the published titles did not receive any critical attention). This concentration intensified in 1991 (60 percent of criticism published focuses on 10 percent of titles, and two-thirds of books were never the subject of a review [Janssen 1997]). A book's chances of being subject to critical attention therefore largely depend on a series of factors, including the book's genre (novel, poetry collection, and so on) and the size and the symbolic capital of the publishing house. The methods of event history analysis, based on regression analyses of longitudinal event data, allow scholars to study the ways in which these factors become differentially relevant over time to an understanding of a text's critical reception (Van Rees and Vermunt 1996).

The Effects of Reception on a Work of Literature

While the effects of consecration on the trajectory and self-perception of an individual author have been studied through interviews in the case of literary prizes (Heinich 1999), the effects of reception on the work itself, and more broadly on the space of possibles, constitute an underexamined field of study within the sociology of literature. Reception shapes the evolution of authors' trajectories: they are beholden to the image that critics and other authorities (editorial, political, literary) reflect back onto them, as well as to the expectations of their peers and the public. The case of Romain Gary, who had to adopt a pseudonym in order to change his literary style (and in order to win the Goncourt Prize for a second time under the pen name Émile Ajar), reveals by contrast the weight of these expectations. Not all cases are so extreme, where the change in writing strategy calls for a strategic dissimulation of the author's identity. But the reception of a work always brings about some kind of readjustment in the author's strategy, which can go as far as a denial of the initial intent, especially when a subversive intent is met with the threat of sanction. And these readjustments can have a knock-on effect on the choice of future writing strategies.

More broadly, reception of a literary work or a cultural product, whether positive or negative, can contribute to redefining the space of possibles. This was the case, for example, with Sartre's famous critique of *La Fin de la nuit* (*The End of the Night*) by the Catholic writer François Mauriac, who was at the time a member of the Académie Française, the highest authority at the heteronomous dominant pole of the field. In 1939, Sartre denounced Mauriac's use of an omniscient narrator by employing Einstein's theory of relativity, accusing the author of confusing the narrator's position with that of God: "there is no more place for a privileged observer in a real novel . . . M. Mauriac has put himself first. He has chosen divine omniscience and omnipotence." He concluded: "God is not an artist. Neither is M. Mauriac" (Sartre 1955, 23). This review had effects not only on Mauriac's trajectory—he adopted the first-person narration in *La Pharisienne* (*A Woman of Pharisees*) in 1941 and then stopped writing novels for a long time—but also on the literary field as a whole, contributing to the obsolescence of the omniscient narrator in French fiction.

These examples show that one cannot claim to write literary or intellectual history without taking into account the processes of reception and their effects. The study of the contentious reception of Ahmadou Kourouma's 1990 novel *Monnè, outrages et défis* (*Monnew: A Novel*) and of the rewriting of his novel, initially meant to condemn colonialism, provides insight into the process by which authors internalize constraints (especially the disuse of committed literature) emanating from Paris, the center of the fracophone area, upon which writers from the former French colonies are still dependent. The study of its reception sheds light on the "postcolonial melancholia" of French consecrating authorities (Ducournau 2010).

While the study of colonial and postcolonial literature enables the reversal of the gaze from the periphery toward the center, the invention of the label "postcolonial" as a brand on the world book market reveals the tensions that run through this literature, between resisting and adapting to the norms of the market, as is illustrated by research on the Booker Prize (Huggan 2001). This consecrating authority, backed by an agri-food multinational corporation with a colonial past, and composed of white male jury members, seated at the British center, designates works "representative" of the periphery, thus establishing a postcolonial canon with Salman Rushdie as its emblematic figure (on the Booker Prize, see also Todd [1996] and Norris [2006]; for similar ambiguities with the Prix des Cinq Continents, see Bedecarré [2020]). The prize is but one link in the publishing chain that produces what Graham Huggan calls "postcolonial exoticism," and ranges from publication in specialized collections, such as Heinemann's "African Writers Series" at Oxford, to book packaging. The authors in question face these constraints as deft strategists, manipulating the rules of the game by skillfully balancing exoticism and critiques of the system, as illustrated by Huggan's analysis of Rushdie's *Midnight's Children*, a book whose distinct receptions—depoliticized in Great Britain, resolutely political in India—attest to this ambiguity. The positioning of postcolonial authors within the world publishing market has been studied in a systematic way using the case studies of Coetzee, Derek Walcott, and Ghose (Brouillette 2007).

The Transnational Circulation of Literary Works

Like literary history, the sociology of literature has favored the nation as the standard geographic space. However, literary value (Lafarge 1983) is also accumulated on an international scale, in a space structured by unequal power relations (Casanova 1999/ 2007). The "denationalization" of literary history raises methodological questions and poses new challenges for the sociology of literature. While comparativism, not only between nations, but also between time periods, remains a major tool for sociological thought (Boschetti 2006, 2010), it must be combined with research on intercultural exchange in order to avoid falling into the trap of methodological nationalism (Sapiro 2010a). Nations were indeed built through constant cultural exchanges and transfers, which a comparative approach must take into account (Espagne and Werner 1990; Thiesse 1999, 2022; for the case of France and Germany, see Espagne [1999]; for Brazil and Argentina, see Sorá [2002]; on foreign literature in France around 1900, see Wilfert-Portal [2008]).

In dialogue with the rising paradigm of "world literature" (Moretti 2000b; Damrosch 2003), scholarship on the transnational circulation of literature constitutes a new, fast-growing research domain within the sociology of literature, paving the way for the sociology of translation (Heilbron 1999; Sapiro 2008; 2015b; see also the research program on the circulation of cultural works outlined by Bourdieu in 1991 [Bourdieu 2023,

83–100]). This research brings up questions about the political and economic constraints that influence international literary exchanges, the relative autonomy from which they benefit, the authoritative bodies that participate in them (publishing houses, literary agencies, embassy cultural services, translation institutes, book fairs, international literature festivals, and so on), and the specific role of intermediaries and mediators (literary agents, rights managers, editors, translators, writers, critics, and so forth). Translation can indeed be considered a social activity whose function, more than just a mediation, is multifaceted. The different aspects of this activity can be divided into three main categories: ideological, economic, and cultural (Sapiro 2016a).

Translation can fulfill ideological functions, such as spreading a doctrine or a worldview. The circulation of literary works has been subject to political constraints under authoritarian regimes, such as fascist Italy or communist countries (Billiani 2007; Rundle 2010; Rundle and Sturge 2010). Ioana Popa (2006, 2010, 2019) undertook research on French translations of literary works from four Communist Bloc countries—Poland, Hungary, Romania, and Czechoslovakia—from 1945 to 1992, adopting a comparative approach both between nations and between time periods. She identified six circuits of cultural transfer, three authorized and three unauthorized. The study of flows of translations revealed a global evolution away from authorized circuits toward unauthorized ones (starting with the 1958 translation of Pasternak's novel *Doctor Zhivago*), an evolution that testifies to the rise of a Western demand for underground literature, with variations linked to the distinct history of each one of these countries.

Translation is also a practice involved in the book market and in this respect it fulfills an economic function. While the economic returns are not the only motivation for publishers, they are no less a real condition for the operation of their business. Certain translations, like certain publications, are above all meant to yield profits. Take, for example, the translations of Harlequin romance novels or international bestsellers such as Dan Brown's *The Da Vinci Code* (2003), which sold 86 million copies worldwide. Genre novels are produced in close relation to the audience's expectations. Harlequin Books, a dominant group in the production of romance, adapts its guidelines for authors to these expectations based on marketing studies. Before it appeared as a book, episodes of *Fifty Shades of Grey* circulated on the internet, and the plot evolved according to readers' reactions, in the same way nineteenth-century authors of serialized novels, such as Eugène Sue, adjusted the story to the readers' comments. A sociological interpretation of the worldwide success of *Fifty Shades of Grey* was proposed by Eva Illouz, who argues that it combines the tradition of the romance, self-help culture, and BDSM (*bondage, discipline, sadism, and masochism*), which symbolically solves current problems in heterosexual relations, thus revealing our social unconscious (Illouz 2014). Economic issues that influence publishing exchanges intensified with globalization (Sapiro 2009c, 2010a). Most titles of genre literature are translated from English, and their reception seems to vary much less across cultures than that of upmarket literature.

If economic considerations often intervene when it comes to translation, because of the highest costs (acquiring translation rights, paying the translator for their work), the circulation of upmarket literary works depends mainly on cultural motivations. Translations played a major role in the construction of national literatures, by forming a body of texts in the national language and by providing literary models (Even-Zohar 1990, 45–96; see also Casanova [2015b]).

Translation also participates in the process of legitimizing literary works (Casanova 2002, 2009, 2021). Having their work translated into a foreign language is a consecration for writers.

It has an impact on their career and may also impact their writing. This is all the more true for authors writing in peripheral languages, when their work is translated into central languages. Some authors enjoy more recognition abroad than in their own country and start adjusting their writing strategies to this foreign audience (Apter 2001). But the probabilities for an author's work to be translated into other languages and achieve international recognition are uneven, depending on the language in which the author writes (central vs. peripheral), their symbolic capital, the symbolic capital of their original publisher, their transnational networks, and the financial aids they can obtain (from the state or from private resources such as philanthropic foundations) (see Sapiro 2012, 2015c).

Conversely, translating the work of a foreign writer who enjoys a certain amount of recognition beyond national borders can constitute a form of self-legitimation for an author. For some authors, especially poets, translating has an experimental dimension, which feeds their own stylistic research (on the translation of poetry, see Blakesley [2018]). Moreover, importing foreign literary works is sometimes, as with past authors, a strategy for subverting dominant literary norms in a national field. For example, Sartre borrowed narrative techniques from Faulkner and Dos Passos, whose works were translated and published by Gallimard (Sartre's publisher) in the 1930s. The French translations of Kafka at the same time also had a deep echo among the young generation of writers, as Nathalie Sarraute acknowledged in *L'Ère du soupçon* (*The Age of Suspicion*, 1956).

For a publisher as well, translation can provide an opportunity to accumulate symbolic capital, as is true for Éditions du Seuil, a Catholic publishing house that built its literary credit on translations, particularly the translations of German writers, such as Günter Grass and Heinrich Böll, before they were awarded the Nobel Prize (Serry 2002). A publisher like Gallimard has accumulated so much symbolic power that it has become a transnational consecrating authority, as attested by its list, which includes more than forty Nobel Laureates in literature (who either originally wrote in French or whose works were translated into French [Sapiro 2015a; in press]). One can thus make the hypothesis that having their work translated with Gallimard enhances an author's chance to win the prestigious prize.

Reception of upmarket literary works is still framed by national categories ("American literature," "French literature," "Italian literature," and so on), despite the growing importance of transnational conglomerates in the global book market, on one hand, and, on the other, the interest since the 1990s for "interstitial" trajectories that escape national categorization, and which were until then disadvantaged for this reason in the transnational literary field (see chapter III): minority authors, émigrés, or postcolonial authors, who hardly fit into these categories (significantly, African writers are classified as a group rather than in national categories) (Sapiro 2015c). Thus, the discourse on globalization as a process of denationalization should be relativized. However, the national categories of perception are more systematically used in the case of writers from peripheral areas, who are often read through "ethnographic" lenses, than in that of authors published in the centers of the transnational literary field, whose writings tend to be received as "universal" (Casanova 1999, 2007; Sapiro 2008, 175–210). The "ethnographic" dimension may turn into exoticism in the case of non-Western authors, the reception of their work participating in the construction or confirmation of a stereotypical representation of their society, as has been shown for female Arab writers, for instance (Jacquemond 2018), in the line of Edward Said's approach of "orientalism" (Said 1978).

Translation into a central language helps "small" national literatures to emerge on the international scene, as was the case with modern Hebrew literature (Sapiro 2002b) or Dutch literature (Heilbron 2008). However, far from being fluid, these imports encounter numerous obstacles, the effects intensifying for authors writing in peripheral languages (Franssen and Kuipers 2015). These obstacles range from the reluctance of publishers to undertake such a costly and risky endeavor to cultural and linguistic obstacles (Sapiro 2010a, 2012, 2015c; Apter 2013). In translation, the text is rewritten according to translating strategies that vary from domestication to foreignization (Toury 1995; Venuti 1998). For instance, in the English translation of Israeli writer David Grossman's *The Smile of the Lamb*, most metaphors were suppressed, probably to make the text more fluent in English. This is a typical example of domestication strategy.

This approach paves the way for a sociology of mediators across cultures (Wilfert-Portal 2002; Popa 2010; Sapiro 2016e) and a sociology of (inter)mediating authorities (Helgesson and Vermeulen 2015; Sapiro 2017; Meyerlarts and Roig-Sanz 2018).

Festivals: A New Object of Study for the Sociology of Literature

While festivals have recently garnered increased attention from researchers, literary festivals remain understudied despite their growing importance in the literary field—with the exception of theater festivals (Fabiani 2008). Literature festivals have been approached from the perspectives of the democratization of culture (Giorgi 2011), cultural consumption (Ommundsen 2009), audience experience (Weber 2018), the construction of continental identity (Ducournau 2019), and their role in the process of recognition and legitimation of works of art and creators (Sapiro 2022).

Since the 1980s the term "festival" has spread as a way to describe public events where literary works are read, commented on, and discussed by specialists, authors, critics, publishers, and translators. Associated with performance arts (theater, music) and visual arts, the festival's form may seem incongruous with reading, the most solitary of today's cultural practices. And yet, from high-society salons to academies, and later to insider circles, such as Mallarmé's Tuesday evenings (*les mardis de Mallarmé*) or the attic of the Brothers Goncourt (Glinoer and Laisney 2013), gatherings dedicated to reading out loud and discussions about literature previously existed, but they remained confined to the private sphere, or to literate gatherings. If the penniless avant-garde invaded the public space of cafés, they strictly selected their members.

The first literary festival in Europe, the Times Cheltenham, was founded in 1949. The Toronto International Festival of Authors came later, in 1974. In France, book festivals first appeared at the margins of the literary field, in little-recognized genres, such as comic books (the Angoulême International comics festival was founded in 1974) and crime fiction (the festival in Reims began in 1986). For these genres, festivals provided a way to gain legitimacy, while their festive dimension broke with the sanctity of "high culture." The Edinburgh International Book Festival (1983), the Melbourne Writers' festival (1986), and the Hay-on-Wye festival of literature and the arts, at first reserved for poetry (1988), were founded at this time. These types of events proliferated starting in the mid-1990s, and they draw large audiences: 90,000 participants across 500 events at Hay-on-Wye in 2009; 400,000 entrances to the Jaipur Literature Festival in 2019. Combining aesthetic standards and strategies to increase the number of visitors, many of these festivals also have a stated political orientation, like the promotion of multiculturalism and internationalism (Giorgi 2011).

The rise of literary festivals was in part due to the confluence of multiple factors: the new forms of promotion developed by the book industry to reach a wider audience (*salons du livre,* book fairs, book festivals), cultural policies in support of reading, and the investment of cultural intermediaries. Literary festivals differ from book fairs and *salons du livre* in their programming, which is to say, a selective offering, at times centered upon a theme, a genre (crime fiction, graphic novels) or a region of the world (Festival America in Vincennes, France), or in their exacting literary taste. They also differ in the amount of time they allocate to public discussion and reading, their convivial settings, and their festivity. The role of festivals in discovering new works of literature is the subject of careful thought by their organizers, which is why such a significant place at these events is given to mediators, such as commentators, critics, translators, or performers. Showcasing the writers in person, as at public readings (Meizoz 2016), festivals involve their physical presence in the construction of the value of their work, using at the same time the fame of some authors—and of other guests, such as musicians or actors—to produce the symbolic value and attractiveness of the whole event. As was the case at previous forms of literary gatherings, festivals perform a ritual function that strengthens *illusio*, namely, the belief in the value of literature; but unlike these previous events, which produced group cohesion among fellow writers, literary festivals aim above all to feed the "lay" public's belief. Festivals also serve to recognize and legitimize debut writers, while for more established authors they help maintain and reinforce their reputation and therefore their symbolic capital.

According to studies conducted on the public attending the Berlin International Literature Festival (Giorgi 2011) and on the festival in France dedicated to contemporary French literature, *Correspondances de Manosque* (Sapiro et al. 2015), these events manage to retain a diverse and returning audience that adheres to their offer. However, despite strategies deployed by organizers to attract the attention of a more popular audience, the events

are only relatively successful at effecting cultural democratization: they bring together a mostly female audience, well endowed
with cultural capital, and whose cultural practices are intense—
which shows how cultural capital persists as a precondition for
reading literature, be it private or public.

Some of these festivals are international, and thus play a
role in the making of world authorship and world literature. A
quantitative and qualitative study of thirty-eight international
literary festivals showed how international literary festivals reflect, even as they shape, the structure of the transnational literary field (Sapiro 2022). International festivals tend indeed to
mirror the unequal conditions of access to world authorship and
the power relations that structure the world market for translations. However, some of them develop strategies to counter
these power relations. They are also more politicized, and try to
construct a more diverse, feminized, and inclusive transnational
public sphere, where writers act as public intellectuals (on the
transnationalization of the public sphere, see Fraser [2007]).
The function of festivals as arenas for an alternative transnational public sphere is confirmed by cases of censorship, such as
the government threat of cancellation of the 2015 Ubud Writers
& Readers Festival, which had programmed events honoring the
victims of the 1965 mass killings in Indonesia, or the pressures
by fundamentalist Islamic communities on the Indian government to prevent Salman Rushdie from coming to the Jaipur festival in 2012 (Weber 2018, 204–7).

All of these mediations, which participate in the process of
production of value of literary works, be it aesthetic, economic,
or ideological, do not provide information on the sociological
profile of the majority of readers, nor do they inform scholars
about readers' experience of reading. Other methods and other
sources must be used in order to do so.

The Sociology of Reading

A solitary and generally silent experience, reading (or listening when a text is read out loud) constitutes a kind of "black box" that makes scientific objectification difficult, beyond individuals' declarations. The sociology and history of reading nevertheless developed in close relationship with studies on books and the printed word, alongside studies on the reception of other art forms and media (for example, studies on museums; for an overview see Charpentier [2006]; Horellou-Lafarge and Segré [2007]). This research domain evolved from using quantitative methods to qualitative approaches, which, since Richard Hoggart's (2009) 1957 study of popular novels, have been renewed.

From Surveys on Reading to Readers' Trajectories

Originating in media studies and publishers' as well as the state's demands (a study was conducted by *INSEE*, the French National Institute of Statistics and Economic Studies, in 1967), research on reading evolved from focusing on the sociography of readers to focusing on reading practices (Donnat 1993; Poulain 1993; Seibel 1995; Robine 2000). Critiques of polling methods and their propensity to impose the problematics and prompt expected answers, paid off: sociological studies on reading use a much more sophisticated questionnaire, but justifiably remain cautious in their interpretations of the results (Fraisse 1993).

In addition to the official studies on the cultural practices of the French conducted in 1973, 1981, 1988–89, and 1997, commissioned by the Ministry of Culture (Donnat and Cogneau 1990; Donnat 1998), more targeted studies on cultural practices were done at the behest of the *Bibliothèque Publique d'Information du Centre Pompidou* and under the umbrella of the *Observatoire France Loisirs*, for example, on the possible connections between reading practices and television-viewing practices (Establet and Felouzis 1992); or on specific populations, such as prisoners (Fabiani and Soldini 1995), metallurgists (Peroni 1988), students (Fraisse 1993), and high school students (Renard 2011). Another (longitudinal) study by a research team showed how schooling shapes literary taste (see Box 8). In a different perspective, a comparative study based on a questionnaire and focusing on "acts of reading" was conducted on the reception of Endre Fejes's *Cimetière de rouille* (*A Generation of Rust*) and Georges Perec's *Les Choses* (*Things: A Story of the Sixties*) in France and in Hungary (Leenhardt and Józsa 1999).

As Bourdieu demonstrates in *La Distinction* (1979), the social hierarchization of the public largely underlies the hierarchy of cultural products. Studies on reading demonstrate the impact of

Box 8. The Role of Schooling in the Development of Literary Taste

While confirming a decline in reading, the longitudinal study of a cohort of 1,200 students conducted by Christian Baudelot, Marie Cartier, and Christine Détrez (1999) also relativizes the meaning of this finding. Most important, the study shows the impact of school on the formation of literary taste. Nineteenth-century French writers constitute the core of this literary culture, at times accompanied by an interest in more contemporary literature. Anglo-American literature, especially mass-market literature, represents close to one-third of what French secondary school pupils read. The most-read writers are Stephen King and Mary Higgins Clark. It is not until they reach *lycée* (high school) that they give more attention to classic German (Kafka, Mann, Zweig), Italian (Buzzatti, Calvino), Russian (Dostoyevsky, Solzhenitsyn, Chekhov. and Tolstoy), and Latin American (Borges, Márquez) authors. At this level of education, school instills a "scholarly" mode of reading that differs from "ordinary" reading by focusing on form and style.

educational capital, gender, and age on the type of book read—the most well-endowed tend to choose texts from the most legitimate categories, women have a marked preference for fiction while men opt for documentary works—but these variations are not automatic, and there are often areas of overlap (Parmentier 1986). The correlation between gender and genre grows when one goes from legitimate literature to popular literary genres, such as romance vs. sci-fi/fantasy, for instance, or to practical books (self-help) vs. books about sport, as has also been observed in a recent study on cultural practices in Australia (Bennett et al. 2022, 32–48).

Quantitative approaches made way for more qualitative research, ranging from the modes of appropriation of literary works to the study of their interpretation based on writers' correspondence (see below) and the study of readers' trajectories (Fossé-Poliak et al. 1999). Other research has focused on the reception of a particular genre, such as romantic fiction (Radway 1984) and the detective novel (Collovald and Neveu 2004). For avant-garde literary works, in particular, access to recognition cannot be understood separately from the development of a specific readership whose social characteristics must be identified, as the example of the Surrealists shows (Bandier 1999). Book clubs also provide an ideal site for observing the modes of sociability around reading and also the exchanges reading gives rise to and their gendered dimension (Albenga 2007).

The Uses of Print and the Evolution of Reading Practices

In order to identify the readership and uses of books, sociologists have adopted sophisticated methods developed by historians who were unable to directly ask the individuals in question. These methods draw on many different sources, such as print runs, distribution, orders, inventories made after deaths, notarial archives, registers from reading rooms (*cabinets de lecture*) and libraries, and writers' correspondence, which enabled scholars to move beyond literary approaches to reception that rely purely on textual analysis and to describe the social conditions and constraints that influence reading practices. The contributions of these studies, which expanded and revised the first *longue durée* perspectives (Lough 1978), are synthesized and discussed in critical overviews (see Chartier [1995]).

The study of reading habits in France from the sixteenth century to the present day, conducted on the basis of sets compiled using legal deposits and the *Bibliographie de la France* (French National Bibliography), shows rather clear trends: the eighteenth century was affected by the decline in Latin and religious texts, the rise of the novel, and interest in nature and faraway cultures.

Print-run data give scholars an idea of the extensive growth in the number of readers from the beginning of the nineteenth century, whose preferred literary form soon became the novel. In France, the average print run for a novel changed from around 1,000–1,500 copies during the Bourbon Restoration to 2,000–3,000 starting in 1840. Except for a few big successes, such as Sir Walter Scott's translated novels, works of contemporary fiction rarely achieved recognition beyond the insular community of well-educated readers. The reading public grew with the launch of serialized novels in 1836 (Lyons 1987). At a time when literacy rates were increasing, reading was no longer a practice exclusively reserved for the dominant classes (Allen 1991). The actual reach of a text was wider than print runs and the geographic distribution of newspapers would lead one to think, as a result of collective reading practices at *veillées* (private evening gatherings), as well as the exchange and/or loaning of books, production of books with serialized novels cut from newspapers, and visits to reading rooms (Thiesse 1984, 49).

Since print runs do not give precise information about reading publics or reading practices, historians of reading have turned to other sources. The study of things like posthumous inventories and notarial archives enabled scholars to observe that novels, travel literature, and books on natural history were replacing the classics in the libraries of nobles and the upper bourgeoisie of the eighteenth century (Roche 1988, 101). Studies of library loans showed a "democratization" of reading beginning in the 1760s: the number of books loaned doubled, library patrons were from more modest backgrounds, and they preferred romance novels over more serious genres.

Publishing archives and catalogs can also provide information on their customers. An analysis of the *bibliothèque bleue*, the most important popular series of colporteurs' books, printed by Garnier, reveals the greater prevalence of books on religion (42.7 percent) as opposed to fiction (28.8 percent) among the readings of the lower classes in the seventeenth century (Chartier 1987a). Robert Darnton (1991, chap. 7), working with the archives of the Swiss publisher and bookseller Société Typographique de Neuchâtel, and studying records of police seizures of books and of book orders, has brought to light the relationship between literary supply and demand in the underground market.

Reading practices are more difficult to study. Although Rolf Engelsing's thesis about the transition during the eighteenth century away from an "intensive" reading habit toward an "extensive" practice that constituted a "reading revolution" has been proven correct, it must be nuanced with more exacting research (Chartier 1987b). Likewise, the evolution away from reading aloud in groups toward reading silently and alone took place at different times depending on the location (cities vs. countryside), social group (literate classes vs. working class), and gender, and varied according to age, genre, and setting (poetry, for example, continued to be read out loud in circles of poets and amateurs).

The problem is thornier still for the modes of appropriation and interpretation that draw the limits of a quantitative approach. Besides literary critics and literary trials, writers' correspondence provides a particularly interesting source for scholars (Allen 1991; Lyon-Caen 2006). This leads us to the question of reading experiences and the modes of appropriation of literary works.

From Identification Theory to Reading Interests

Theories of reception have been shaped by the idea of two publics: on the one hand, the literate readers, characterized by detachment and ability to distance themselves from the text; on the other, working-class readers, women, and youth, whose relationship to reading was conceived of as based on identification (Molinié and Viala 1993; Sapiro 2011b). Indeed, while the discourse on the harmful effects of "bad readings" goes at least as far back as the invention of the printing press, with the spread of literacy in the nineteenth century, the old distinction between literate and illiterate changed: "the criteria of esthetic disposition (knowing what to read and how) came to replace the criteria of practical proficiency (knowing how to read)" (Thiesse 1984, 518).

The distinction between "serious readings" and "entertaining readings" that held sway until then reflected above all the categories of books read, primarily pitting essays against novels. This categorization became muddled in France during the July Monarchy: the consecration of the genre of the novel happened alongside its assimilation with sociological studies, as a number of writers having opted for the Realist vein, from Balzac to Eugène Sue, so claimed. In response to critics who saw the novel as a product of obscene entertainment, Sue set out to exhibit proof of "serious" readings of his *Mystères de Paris* (*The*

Mysteries of Paris) by judges, doctors, and philanthropists, in the French newspaper *Le Journal des débats* (Thiesse 1980). During the same period, an "aesthete" reading, different from the "serious" and "entertaining" reading habits, asserted itself in France with the theory of "art for art's sake" and the reception of Kantian aesthetics, which defined aesthetic pleasure as disinterested (Sapiro 2011b, 168–72, 285–305).

The "serious" reading attitude toward literary works can be seen in readers' letters, as studied by Judith Lyon-Caen (2006): their interests are diverse, ranging from education to political uses of the text (by philanthropists and militant workers), the serious reading always taking precedence over entertainment. While it is risky to make inferences about these practices as a whole based solely on these reconstructions, which in part have to do with the presentation of self (in Erving Goffman's sense of staging), they nevertheless provide just as much information about the reception of these novels as if they were social inquiries and documentary evidence. Without being confused with reality, fiction provides an interpretive framework for the way the social world functions, linking lived experience to social representations internalized by readers, or revealing little-known aspects of society to the reader, eliciting feelings of pity and indignation, without this process necessarily entailing ethical or ideological adhesion to the values represented.

The notion of identification therefore appears overly reductive for describing these reading experiences, which, even when relating fiction to the reader's life experience, serve more to compare, situate, analyze, and make generalizations (by elaborating social types or destinies), in a dual process of a self-socioanalysis and appraisal of the fiction in terms of verisimilitude and morals. The same applies to so-called "entertainment" reading, for which the representation in scholarship fluctuates between the frameworks of identification and escapism.

Although testimonies of the reading practices of autodidact readers show an eclecticism that combines erudition with books for a large audience, they are associated with the latter category, which became a stigma of their cultural unworthiness (Hébrard 1990, 550). Besides women, the underprivileged readers from lower classes were suspected of being the receptacle for these "bad books" that, according to their critics, fuel selfish interests and arouse the most vile instincts. During the July Monarchy, the harshest critics of the novel, a genre that was seen as the worst of "bad books," feared that it fomented ambitions of upward social mobility that would threaten the established order, especially since these books reached what was known as the "intellectual proletariat" (penniless students, monitors, supervisors, notary or court bailiff clerks, aspiring writers) and the urban working-class elite (typographers and printers). Confirming the importance of the theme of social mobility in the reception of these novels, the study of the letters sent to Balzac and Sue shows that their readers drew from their work in order to analyze experiences of downward social mobility or to understand the obstacles to their own dreams of upward social mobility, rather than to seek encouragement (Lyon-Caen 2006).

The invention of educational books, which gave rise to a new publishing market, led to a strict separation between popular culture and school culture (Hébrard 1990, 547). But school culture was in and of itself hierarchical, divided into two levels of instruction—the secondary, reserved for children of the bourgeoisie (it remained the case until the mandating of free admissions in 1931) and the primary, which became the school of the people (with the law of 1882 on compulsory education). Literature does not have the same function at each level: at the primary level, it is taught to inculcate moral values and principles, and at the secondary level it is taught to cultivate the mind and reflection. There was also a gendered division, which pitted "serious" masculine readings (politics especially) against "frivolous" feminine readings (serialized novels). Thus, a tripartite hierarchy of the elite's disinterested practices, the moral and social utility of serious readings for the working and middle classes, and texts read for entertainment such as serialized novels, relegated to the bottom of the ladder, replaced the dichotomy between learned and popular culture. This hierarchy persisted at least until the 1950s, when the growth of the image helped relativize the representations of books as dangerous (A.-M. Chartier and Hébrard 2000) and allowed publishers to develop a discourse about reading as a superior cultural practice, with educational value, compared to film or television, without the disappearance of the opposition between "aesthete" and "entertainment" reading from sociocultural classifications.

These representations have been, on the contrary, strengthened just as much at the conservative pole as at the Marxist pole of the intellectual field and the space of moral entrepreneurs by the flourishing of cultural industries and the emergence of a so-called "mass" culture. The Frankfurt School saw mass-market cultural products as the means to mystify the masses, a new "opium of the people." However, in *The Uses of Literacy*, Richard Hoggart (2009) proposes the notion of "*oblique*" reading to describe working-class reading practices. Anne-Marie Thiesse (1984) has shown that the identification with characters from the fictional universe of the serialized novels was unlikely for readers from underprivileged classes; she prefers talking about "conventional realism" and "distancing oneself from the real world." These studies highlight the fact that the underprivileged readers internalize domination and thus trivialize and discredit their own reading practices instead of valuing them. Far from denying the stereotypical and repetitive nature of certain cultural productions meant for the largest audience, this is a reminder that "alienation, if there was indeed alienation, could not be caused by these novels since it is built into a social class's relationship to the world, a class who is denied the theoretical mastery of its (in this case cultural) practices" (Thiesse, 1984, 49). Interestingly enough, it is less these productions than the way they are consumed to which the alienating effects are attributed, as is demonstrated by the idea that literate readers are protected by their ability to absorb these novels without taking them literally. The same distinction exists today about television.

Identification most often operates within the framework that Genette (1991/1993) calls the "fictional pact," that is, the convention that consists of the reader entering a fictional world to play the game, to take it seriously as if it were real, all while knowing that it is an illusion. One of the characteristics of the process of fictional immersion lies in the fact that it is a "split state of mind," as Jean-Marie Schaeffer (1999, 325/2010, 298) argues: "it detaches us from ourselves, or, rather it detaches us from our own proper representations, in that it produces them according to the mode of the 'as if,' thus introducing a distance from ourselves to ourselves." More than a simple opposition between detachment and identification, research on readers' trajectories highlights the diversity of practices and "reading interests": for learning, entertainment, practical advice, religious devotion, and so on, which can coexist in one person, including aesthete reading (Mauger and Poliak 1998).

The theories developed by new branches of philosophy, which see reading fiction as a democratic resource in that it enables the peaceful cohabitation of different groups in society, have yet to be empirically grounded, whether it is the purging of passions through Aristotelian catharsis, or the exercise of empathic skills foregrounded in theories of care (and in particular by Martha Nussbaum), or symbolization as a way of enriching axiological thought. Research methods for studying this could be considered by observing debates between writers and their audience at different public events or during exchanges among readers in private circles.

From the sociology of intermediaries of the book production network and consecrating authorities to the social and political stakes of critical reception, as well as the sociology of reading practices and experiences, various avenues for future research, which deserve further in-depth study, have been advanced by the sociology of literature. Other fields of study have yet to be explored. The development of electronic media, which constitutes a kind of "return" to writing after television, poses new challenges for the study of reading practices and the social uses of reading. Yet, despite the development of writers' websites, there is not a great deal of work being done on online literary publishing and reading practices on the internet. The use of social media, as well as the collective mobilizations in what has been called by its detractors "cancel culture," offers a new site of observation of the ethical and political judgments on works of art and literature, the discussions they spark about reading practices, and the collective regulation of these practices (for instance, partial "cancellation" such as erasing the name of author J. K. Rowling on *Harry Potter* volumes). They also raise anew the question of the author's function (to cite Foucault) and personae in the reception process (Sapiro 2020b).

Conclusion

Still poorly institutionalized despite an already well-established tradition, the sociology of literature is nevertheless poised to reinvigorate the thinking in the two disciplines to which it belongs. This is the case for the sociology of professions, the sociology of education, the analysis of social relations (class, gender, race) and of individual and collective strategies, the sociology of the media, and economic sociology. The sociology of literature has also contributed to the emergence of new fields, such as the sociology of art and culture, of publishing, of translation, and of international cultural exchanges, illuminating the study of phenomena such as globalization, notably by resituating them within the *longue durée*.

In literary studies, the sociological approach has made it possible to move away from the internal analysis of literary works by situating them among other social discourses, by bringing to light the representations and values they convey, and by relating them to the conditions of their production (at the individual and collective levels), while at the same time reflecting on the mediations between these external determinants and the text. The sociology of literature is in dialogue with discourse analysis, genetic criticism, and works focused on individual writers, as well as with those that interrogate the relationship between literature and politics, literature and law, or literature and morality, and with postcolonial studies and studies in world literature.

The mediations between the text and its context operate, as we have seen, on several levels. From the point of view of the conditions of production, they reside in the structure of the field (orthodoxy vs. heresy), its literary institutions (authors societies, academies, prizes), the competing conceptions of the social role of the writer ("art for art's sake" vs. "committed literature"), and professional ideology. From the point of view of creation, the principal mediations are the space of possibles and the work of formalization, which is informed by that space and its history, as well as by the writer's social trajectory. Finally, the existence of an aesthetic critical judgment—that is to say, one that is relatively autonomous from the moral, political, or social judgment of literary works—illustrates the effect of mediation that the field exerts at the level of reception: aesthetic judgment, centered on form, is opposed to heteronomous judgments that evaluate literature according to the ideological or economic functions (sales) it fulfills.

New fields of research in the sociology of literature have been opened up around processes of selection, reception, and the international circulation of works—to which have been added, following the work of Edward Said (1978) and postcolonial studies, the question of the manifestations and effects of colonialism in literature (for example, on the reconfiguration of the francophone literary space after independence). Still, some of the avenues explored in the 1970s have been unfortunately overlooked, such as the mediation exercised by educational institutions in the transmission of literary models and, more generally, their role in forming the canon. The relationships between literature and the other arts also remain to be explored.

In bringing this panorama to a close, it seems clear that if many avenues of research have been opened, there are many more yet to be made. New perspectives are emerging on the material conditions of the writer's profession, on the role and sociological profile of literary agents, on the comparative history of genres and subgenres, on translation and the international circulation of works, on the building of literary reputations, and on the study of new forms of intermediation, such as festivals, and new media, such as the internet. As for quantitative methods, in addition to geometric analysis, the utility of which has already been demonstrated, network analysis and event history analysis open up new possibilities for exploring the inner workings of the world of letters and those of fictional universes: just as the geographical space in which Frédéric Moreau, the protagonist of Flaubert's *Sentimental Education*, moves through life can be mapped, the structure of his network of relations can also be modeled. And digital methods of "distant reading" enrich our understanding of literary evolution. With regard to the experience of reading fiction, we need to devise investigative methods that would empirically ground the theoretical reflections on fiction's capacity to promote the development of empathetic capacities and "democratic" virtues.

Notes

Introduction

1. The "space of possibles" refers to the cultural forms, embodied in cultural works, that are available in a given social configuration (Bourdieu 1992, 326–32; 1996, 234–39).

2. On the misunderstandings between the two disciplines, see Meizoz (2004, 17).

3. These angles from sociology differentiate the present book from overviews that preceded it (see, for instance, Dirkx 2000; Aron and Viala 2006).

4. Following Moretti's notion of "distant reading" (Moretti 2013) and his pioneer investigations with the Stanford Lab; see, for instance, Flanders and Jannadis (2018), Underwood (2019), and the work published by the *Journal of Cultural Analytics*.

Chapter I

1. In the first half of the nineteenth century, the term "liberal" referred to a political movement in Europe that promoted the extension of freedom to all areas, especially the press, all while limiting the right to vote to the higher classes (aristocracy, bourgeoisie, and the professions). In France, the liberal movement formed in opposition to Napoleon and would later contribute to the revolution of 1830 and to the fall of the Bourbon monarchy. Madame de Staël (d. 1817) belonged to the liberal opposition under Napoleon.

2. The term "republicans" designated at the time a left-wing liberal political current that promoted a republican (democratic) form of government against the monarchy.

3. This old meaning of "race" is quite different from the pseudo-biological definition of racial theory, which began developing at the same time in a pseudo-evolutionary perspective.

4. "Positivist history" in France means a history that is attached to facts and events (usually political ones), rather than to processes and problematics, as developed by the Annales School in the interwar period.

5. Bourdieu planned to fully develop his field theory in a book that he was not able to complete before his death, but which was reconstructed in a recent publication (Bourdieu 2022).

6. On the benefits of field theory to the sociology of literature, see Boschetti (2006) and Sapiro (2021). For uses of the concept in national contexts other than France, see, for instance, on Germany, Joch and Wolf (2005), Tommek and Bogdal (2012), and Tommek (2015); on Italy, Baldini (2023); and on China, Hockx (2019).

7. It is the first of the three pitfalls of functionalism singled out by Merton (1968, 73–117): functional unity of the system, which presents the practices and beliefs as functional not only to the whole but also to each of the individuals that compose it; universal functionalism, which assigns to all the elements of a system positive functions (ignoring the inertia of past elements, which do not fulfill the function anymore); and indispensability, which confuses the element with its function.

Chapter II

1. Latin term for the old class of erudite people working in universities, which were then controlled by the Church. Today, it is mostly used ironically to describe a stuffy old scholar. [Translators' note.]

2. The first of these laws made writing an act of free enterprise (freeing it from guilds and trade unions); the second further strengthened copyright protections. [Translators' note.]

3. On forms of sociability, see Glinoer and Laisney (2013).

4. Civil service in the French context includes being a member of the professoriate. [Translators' note.]

Chapter III

1. Most probably due to its widespread use in Nazi Germany.

2. The fate of the aristocracy in Proust's novel is an example of déclassement, a common sociological term. [Translators' note.]

3. Sometimes translated as "putting-into-form." [Translators' note.]

4. On the Bildungsroman, see Moretti (2000a).

5. For an introduction to the uses of digital methods in the humanities, see Flanders and Jannadis (2018). For examples of empirical work based on these methods, see the *Journal of Cultural Analytics*.

6. In France, the agrégation is a competitive exam for entering the civil service as a teacher in the public secondary education system. [Translators' note.]

7. "Beur" refers to the children of North African immigrants born in France. Derived from the pejorative slang word for "Arab" (arabe), the term was used primarily in the 1980s and 1990s by writers (as well as filmmakers and activists) to articulate a specific artistic and political identity. [Translators' note.]

8. In her last book on translation and domination, Pascale Casanova (2015b) shows that the same process occurred earlier, starting in the sixteenth century, for the French language, whose literary development was anchored in translations from Latin, then the dominant language.

9. As Emily Apter (2006) shows in the first part of her book, *The Translation Zone.*

Chapter IV

1. https://www.ala.org/advocacy/bbooks/frequentlychallenged books/decade2019.

References

Note: ARSS = Actes de la recherche en sciences sociales.

Abiola Irele, Francis. 2011. *The Negritude Moment: Explorations in Francophone African and Caribbean Literature and Thought.* Trenton, NJ: Africa World Press.

Abbott, Andrew. 1988. *The System of Professions: An Essay on the Division of Expert Labor.* Chicago: University of Chicago Press.

Adorno, Theodor W., and Paul Kottman. 1991. *Notes to Literature,* Volume 1. Edited by R. Tiedemann; translated by W. Nicholson. Rev. ed. New York: Columbia University Press.

Ahearne, Jeremy, and John Speller, eds. "Pierre Bourdieu and the Literary Field." *Paragraph* 35, no. 1.

Albenga, Viviane. 2007. "Le Genre de 'la distinction.' La construction réciproque du genre, de la classe et de la légitimité littéraire dans les pratiques collectives de lecture." *Sociétés & Représentations* 24, no. 2: 161–76.

Allen, James Smith. 1981. *Popular French Romanticism: Authors, Readers and Books in the 19th Century.* Syracuse, NY: Syracuse University Press.

———. 1991. *In the Public Eye: a History of Reading in Modern France, 1800–1940.* Princeton: Princeton University Press.

Althusser, Louis, Etienne Balibar, Roger Establet, Pierre Macherey, and Jacques Rancière. 1965. *Lire le Capital.* Paris: Maspero.

———. 1970. *Reading Capital*. Translated by Ben Brewster. London: NLB.

Anderson, Benedict. 1983. *Imagined Communities: Reflections on the Origin and Spread of Nationalism*. Rev. ed. London: Verso.

André, Marie-Odile. 2000. *Les Mécanismes de classicisation d'un écrivain. Le cas de Colette*. Metz: Centre d'Études Linguistiques des Textes et des Discours.

Angenot, Marc. 1989. *1889. Un état du discours social*. Quebec: Le Préambule.

———. 2004. "Social Discourse Analysis: Outlines of a Research Project." *Yale Journal of Criticism* 17, no. 2: 199–215.

Anheier, Helmut K., Jurgen Gerhards, and Frank P. Romo. 1995. "Forms of Capital and Social Structure in Cultural Fields: Examining Bourdieu's Social Topography." *American Journal of Sociology* 100, no. 4: 859–903.

Anheim, Étienne, and Antoine Lilti, eds. 2010. "Savoirs de la littérature." *Annales. Histoire, science sociales* 65, no. 2.

Apter, Emily. 2001. "On Translation in a Global Market." *Public Culture* 13, no. 1: 1–12.

———. 2006. *The Translation Zone: A New Comparative Literature*. Princeton: Princeton University Press.

———. 2013. *Against World Literature: On the Politics of Untranslatability*. London: Verso.

Aron, Paul. 1995. *La Littérature prolétarienne*. Bruxelles: Labor.

———. 2005. "La Littérature en Belgique francophone de 1930–1960. Débats et problèmes autour d'un 'sous-champ.'" In *Intégrité intellectuelle. Mélanges en l'honneur de Joseph Jurt*, edited by Michael Einfalt, Ursula Erzgräber, and Ottmar Ette, 417–28. Memmingen: Universitätsverlag Winter Heidelberg.

———, and Alain Viala. 2006. *Sociologie de la littérature*. Paris: PUF "Que sais-je?"

Baldini, Anna. 2023. *A regola d'arte. Storia e geografia del campo letterario italiano (1902–1936)*. Macerata, Italy: Quodlibet Studio.

Bandier, Norbert. 1999. *Sociologie du surréalisme. 1924–1929*. Paris: La Dispute.

Baudelot, Christian, Marie Cartier, and Christine Détrez. 1999. *Et pourtant ils lisent . . .* Paris: Seuil.

Baudorre, Philippe, Dominique Rabaté, and Dominique Viart, eds. 2007. *Littérature et sociologie*. Paris: Presses Universitaires de Bordeaux.

Becker, Howard. 2008. *Art Worlds, 25th Anniversary Edition*. Berkeley: University of California Press [1982].

Bedecarré, Madeline. 2017. "Apprendre à écrire? Des formations de *creative writing* aux États-Unis aux masters de création littéraire." In *Profession écrivain*, edited by Gisèle Sapiro and Cécile Rabot, 154–67. Paris: CNRS Éditions.

———. 2020. "Prizing Francophonie into Existence: The Usurpation of World Literature by the Prix des Cinq Continents." *Journal of World Literature* 5, no. 2: 298–319.

Benaglia, Cecilia. 2020. *Engagements de la forme. Une sociolecture des œuvres de Carlo Emilio Gadda et Claude Simon*. Paris: Garnier.

Bennett, Tony, David Carter, Modesto Gayo, Michelle Kelly, and Greg Noble, eds. 2022. *Fields, Capitals, Habitus: Australian Culture, Inequalities and Social Divisions*. London: Routledge.

Bensa, Alban, and François Pouillon, eds. 2012. *Terrains d'écrivains. Littérature et ethnographie*. Toulouse: Anacharsis.

Bhabha, Homi K. 2012. *The Location of Culture*. 2nd ed. London: Routledge [1994].

Bidou, Catherine. 1997. *Proust sociologue. De la maison aristocratique au salon bourgeois. Intégrité intellectuelle*. Paris: Descartes & Cie.

Bied, Robert. 1991. "La Condition d'auteur." In *Histoire de l'édition française*, vol. 2, edited by Roger Chartier and Henri-Jean Martin, 773–99. Paris: Fayard/Promodis.

Billiani, Francesca, ed. 2007. *Modes of Censorship and Translation: National Contexts and Diverse Media*. Manchester, UK: St. Jerome.

Blakesley, Jacob, ed. 2018. *Sociologies of Poetry Translation: Emerging Perspectives*. London: Bloomsbury.

Bohmer, Elleke. 2015. *Indian Arrivals 1870–1915: Networks of British Empire*. Oxford: Oxford University Press.

Boltanski, Luc. 1975. "Pouvoir et impuissance. Projet intellectuel et sexualité dans le journal d'Amiel." *ARSS* 5–6: 80–108.

Boschetti, Anna. 1985. *Sartre et "Les Temps Modernes." Une entreprise intellectuelle*. Paris: Minuit.

———. 1988. *The Intellectual Enterprise: Sartre and Les Temps Modernes*. Translated by Richard C. McCleary. Evanston, IL: Northwestern University Press.

———. 1991. "Légitimité littéraire et stratégies éditoriales." In *Histoire de l'édition française*, vol. 4 : *Le Livre concurrencé 1900–1950*, edited by Roger Chartier and Henri-Jean Martin, 511–50. Paris: Fayard/Promodis.

———. 1994. "Des revues et des hommes." *La Revue des revues* 18: 51–65.

———. 2001. *La Poésie partout. Apollinaire, homme-époque (1898–1918)*. Paris: Seuil.

———. 2003. "Le 'formalisme réaliste' d'Olivier Cadiot. Une réponse à la question des possibles et du rôle de la recherche littéraire aujourd'hui." In *L'Écrivain, le savant et le philosophe*, edited by Eveline Pinto, 235–50. Paris: Publications de la Sorbonne.

———. 2006. "Bourdieu's Work on Literature: Contexts, Stakes and Perspectives." *Theory, Culture & Society*, 23, no. 6: 135–55.

———, ed. 2010. *L'Espace culturel transnational*. Paris: Nouveau Monde Éditions.

———. 2012. "How Field Theory Can Contribute to Knowledge of World Literary Space." *Paragraph* 35, no. 1: 10–29.

———. 2014. *"Ismes." Du réalisme au postmodernisme*. Paris: CNRS Éditions.

Bouju, Emmanuel. 2002. *Réinventer la littérature. Démocratisation et modèles romanesques dans l'Espagne post-franquiste*. Toulouse: PUM, Les Hespérides.

———, Alexandre Gefen, Guiomar Hautcoeur, Marielle Macé, eds. 2007. *Littérature et exemplarité*. Rennes: Presses Universitaires Rennes.

Bourdieu, Pierre. 1971a. "Le marché des biens symboliques." *L'Année sociologique* 22: 49–126.

———. 1971b. "Une interprétation de la théorie de la religion selon Max Weber." *Archives européennes de sociologie* 12, no. 1: 3–21.

———. 1977. "La Production de la croyance." *ARSS* 13: 3–43.

———. 1979. *La Distinction. Critique sociale du jugement*. Paris: Minuit.

———. 1980. "The Production of Belief: Contribution to an Economy of Symbolic Goods." *Media, Culture & Society* 2, no. 3: 261–93.

———. 1983. "The Field of Cultural Production, or: The Economic World Reversed." *Poetics* 12, nos. 4–5: 311–56.

———. 1984a. *Questions de sociologie*. Paris: Minuit [1980].

———. 1984b. *Distinction: A Social Critique of the Judgement of Taste*. Translated by Richard Nice. Cambridge, MA: Harvard University Press.

———. 1985a. "Existe-t-il une littérature belge? Limites d'un champ et frontières politiques." *Études de lettres* 3: 3–6. Reprinted in Bourdieu 2023, 101–4.

———. 1985b. "The Market of Symbolic Goods." *Poetics* 14, nos. 1–2: 13–44.

———. 1986. "L'Illusion biographique." *ARSS* 62–63: 69–72.

———. 1991a. "First Lecture: Social Space and Symbolic Space: Introduction to a Japanese Reading of Distinction." Translated by Gisele Sapiro and Brian McHale. *Poetics Today* 12, no. 4: 627–38.

———. 1991b. "Le Champ littéraire." *ARSS* 89: 4–46.

———. 1992. *Les Règles de l'art. Genèse et structure du champ littéraire.* Paris: Seuil.

———. 1993a. *Sociology in Question.* Translated by Richard Nice. Thousand Oaks, CA: Sage Publications.

———. 1993b. *The Field of Cultural Production.* Edited and introduced by Randal Johnson. Cambridge, UK: Polity Press.

———.1994. "Pour une science des œuvres." In *Raisons pratiques. Sur la théorie de l'action,* 59–98. Paris: Seuil.

———. 1996. *The Rules of Art: Genesis and Structure of the Literary Field.* Translated by Susan Emanuel. Stanford: Stanford University Press.

———. 1998a. *Practical Reason: On the Theory of Action.* Translated by Randal Johnson. Stanford: Stanford University Press.

———.1998b. *La Domination masculine.* Paris: Seuil.

———.1999a. "Une révolution conservatrice dans l'édition." *ARSS* 126–27: 3–28.

———. 1999b. "The Social Conditions of the International Circulation of Ideas." in *Bourdieu: A Critical Reader,* edited by Richard Shusterman, 220–28. Hoboken, NJ: Wiley-Blackwell.

———. 2002a. "Les Conditions sociales de la circulation internationale des idées." *ARSS* 145: 3–8.

———. 2002b. *Masculine Domination.* Translated by Randal Johnson. Stanford: Stanford University Press.

———. 2008. "A Conservative Revolution in Publishing." *Translation Studies* 1, no. 2: 123–53.

———. 2017. "The Biographical Illusion (1986)." In *Biography in Theory,* edited by Wilhelm Hemecker and Edward Saunders, 210–16. Berlin: De Gruyter.

———. 2022. *Microcosmes. Théorie des champs.* Edited by Jérôme Bourdieu and Franck Poupeau. Paris: Raisons d'Agir.

———. 2023. *Impérialismes. Circulation internationale des idées et luttes pour l'universel.* Edited by Jérôme Bourdieu, Franck Poupeau, and Gisèle Sapiro. Paris: Raisons d'Agir.

Bouveresse, Jacques. 2008. *La Connaissance de l'écrivain. Sur la littérature, la vérité et la vie.* Paris: Agone.

Braun, Rebecca, Tobias Boes, and Emily Spiers, eds. 2020. *Oxford*

Handbook of World Authorship. Oxford: Oxford University Press, 149–64.

Brière, Emilie, and Alexandre Gefen, eds. 2013. "Fiction et démocratie," special issue, *Fixxion. Revue critique de fiction contemporaine* 6, www.revue-critique-de-fixxion-francaise-contemporaine.org/rcffc.

Brouillette, Sarah. 2007. *Postcolonial Writers and the Global Literary Marketplace*. London: Palgrave.

Brun, Eric. 2014. *L'Avant-garde totale. Le mouvement situationniste dans les arts et la politique des années 1950–1960*. Paris: CNRS Éditions.

Burt, Ronald. 1992. *Structural Holes: The Social Structure of Competition*. Cambridge, MA: Harvard University Press.

Casanova, Pascale. 1997. *Beckett, l'abstracteur*. Paris: Seuil.

———.1999. *La République mondiale des lettres*. Paris: Seuil.

———. 2002. "Consécration et accumulation de capital littéraire. La traduction comme échange inégal." *ARSS* 144: 7–20.

———. 2007. *The World Republic of Letters*. Translated by Malcolm DeBevoise. Cambridge, MA: Harvard University Press [2004].

———. 2009. "Consecration and Accumulation of Literary Capital. Translation as Unequal Exchange." In *Critical Readings in Translation Studies*, edited by Mona Baker, 285–303. London: Routledge.

———. 2011a. "Combative Literatures." *New Left Review* 72: 123–34.

———, ed. 2011b. *Des littératures combatives. L'internationale des nationalismes littéraires*. Paris: Raisons d'Agir.

———. 2011c. *Kafka en colère*. Paris: Seuil.

———. 2015a. *Kafka, Angry Poet*. Translated by Chris Turner. London: Seagull Books.

———. 2015b. *La Langue mondiale. Traduction et domination*. Paris: Seuil, 2015.

———. 2020. *Samuel Beckett: Anatomy of a Literary Revolution*. Translated by Gregory Elliott. London: Verso.

Cassagne, Albert. 1997. *La Théorie de l'art pour l'art en France chez les derniers romantiques et les premiers réalistes*. Paris: Champ Vallon [1906].

Charle, Christophe. 1977. "Situation sociale et position spatiale. Géographie sociale du champ littéraire parisien." *ARSS* 13: 45–59.

———. 1979. *La Crise littéraire à l'époque du naturalisme. Roman. Théâtre. Politique*. Paris: Presses de l'École Normale Supérieure.

———. 1982. "Situation du champ littéraire." *Littérature* 44: 8–21.

———. 1990. *Naissance des "intellectuels" 1880–1900.* Paris: Minuit.

———. 1996. *Les Intellectuels en Europe au XIXe siècle. Essai d'histoire comparée.* Paris: Seuil.

———. 2015. *Birth of the Intellectuals: 1880–1900.* Translated by G. M. Goshgarian. Cambridge, UK: Polity.

Charpentier, Isabelle. 1994. "De corps à corps—Réceptions croisées d'Annie Ernaux." *Politix* 27: 45–75.

———, ed. 2006. *Comment sont reçues les œuvres.* Paris: Creaphis.

———. 2013. *Le Rouge aux joues. Virginité, interdits sexuels et rapports de genre au Maghreb.* Saint-Étienne, France: Publications de l'Université de Saint-Étienne.

Chartier, Anne-Marie, and Jean Hébrard. 2000. *Discours sur la lecture (1880–2000).* Paris: Fayard [1989].

Chartier, Roger. 1987a. *Lectures et lecteurs dans la France d'Ancien Régime.* Paris: Seuil.

———, ed. 1987b. *Les Usages de l'imprimé (XVe–XIXe siècle).* Paris: Fayard.

———. 1988. "Du livre au livre." *Réseaux* 6, no. 31: 39–67.

———. 1994. *The Order of Books: Readers, Authors, and Libraries in Europe between the 14th and 18th Centuries.* Stanford: Stanford University Press.

———, ed. 1995. *Histoires de la lecture. Un bilan des recherches.* Paris: IMEC/Éditions de la MSH.

———. 1996. *Culture écrite et société. L'Ordre des livres (XIVe–XVIIIe siècle).* Paris: Albin Michel.

———, ed. 2014. *The Culture of Print: Power and the Uses of Print in Early Modern Europe.* Translated by Lydia G. Cochrane. Princeton: Princeton University Press.

Childress, Clayton. 2019. *Under the Cover: The Creation, Production, and Reception of a Novel.* Princeton: Princeton University Press.

Collovald, Annie, and Eric Neveu. 2004. *Lire le noir. Enquête sur les lecteurs de récits policiers.* Paris: Éditions de la BPI–Centre Georges Pompidou.

Corse, Sarah. 1997. *Nationalism and Literature: The Politics of Culture in Canada and the United States.* Cambridge: Cambridge University Press.

Coser, Louis, Charles Kadushin, and Walter Powell. 1982. *Books: The Culture and Commerce of Publishing.* New York: Basic Books.

Cottenet, Cécile. 2017. *Literary Agents in the Transatlantic Book Trade: American Fiction, French Rights, and the Hoffman Agency.* New York: Routledge.

Damrosch, David. 2003. *What Is World Literature?* Princeton: Princeton University Press.

Darnton, Robert. 1982. *The Literary Underground of the Old Regime.* Cambridge, MA: Harvard University Press.

———. 1991. *Édition et sédition. L'Univers de la littérature clandestine au XVIII*ᵉ *siècle.* Paris: Gallimard.

———. 1992. *Gens de lettres, gens du livre.* Paris: Odile Jacob.

———. 1995. *The Corpus of Clandestine Literature in France, 1769–1789.* New York: W. W. Norton.

———. 1996. *The Forbidden Best-Sellers of Pre-Revolutionary France.* New York: W. W. Norton.

David, Jérôme. 2010. "Une 'réalité à mi-hauteur.' Exemplarités littéraires et généralisations savantes au XIXᵉ siècle." *Annales. Histoire, science sociales* 65, no. 2: 263–90.

Deleuze, Gilles, and Félix Guattari. 1975. *Kafka. Pour une littérature mineure.* Paris: Minuit.

———. 1986. *Kafka: Toward a Minor Literature.* Translated by Dana Polan. Minneapolis: University of Minnesota Press.

De Marneffe, Daphné, and Benoît Denis, eds. 2006. *Les Réseaux littéraires.* Brussels: Le Cri.

Denis, Benoît. 2000. *Littérature et engagement de Pascal à Sartre.* Paris: Seuil.

De Nooy, Wouter. 1991. "Social Networks and Classification in Literature." *Poetics* 20: 507–37.

———. 2003. "Fields and Networks: Correspondence Analysis and Social Network Analysis in the Framework of Field Theory." *Poetics* 31: 305–27.

Desan, Philippe, Priscilla Parkhurst Ferguson, and Wendy Griswold, eds. 1988. *Literature and Social Practice.* Chicago: University of Chicago Press.

Détrez, Christine. 2012. *Femmes du Maghreb, une écriture à soi.* Paris: La Dispute.

Diaz, José-Luis. 2007. *L'Écrivain imaginaire. Scénographies auctoriales à l'époque romantique.* Paris: Honoré Champion.

Dirkx, Paul. 2000. *Sociologie de la littérature.* Paris: Armand Colin.

Donnat, Olivier. 1993. *Les Français face à la culture.* Paris: La Découverte.

———, ed. 1998. *Les Pratiques culturelles des Français. Enquête 1997.* Paris: La Documentation Française.

———, and Denis Cogneau. 1990. *Les Pratiques culturelles des Français. 1973–1989.* Paris: La Découverte/La Documentation Française.

Dozo, Björn-Olav. 2011. *Mesures de l'écrivain. Profil socio-littéraire et capital relationnel dans l'entre-deux-guerres en Belgique francophone.* Liège: Presses Universitaires de Liège–Sciences Humaines.

Dragomir, Lucia. 2007. *Une institution littéraire transnationale à l'Est. L'Exemple roumain.* Paris: Belin.

Dubois, Jacques. 1997. *Pour Albertine.* Paris: Seuil.

———. 2005. *L'Institution littéraire.* Brussels: Labor [1978].

———. 2007. *Une sociologie romanesque.* Paris : La Découverte.

———, and Paul Durand. 1988. "Champ littéraire et classes de textes." *Littérature* 70 (May): 5–23.

Dubois, Sébastien. 2008. "Mesurer la réputation. Reconnaissance et renommée des poètes contemporains." *Histoire et mesure* 23, no. 2: 103–43.

———. 2009. "Entrer au panthéon littéraire." *Revue française de sociologie* 50: 3–29.

———, and Pierre François. 2013. "Career Paths and Hierarchies in the Pure Pole of the Literary Field: The Case of Contemporary Poetry." *Poetics* 41: 501–23.

Duchet, Claude, ed. 1979. *Sociocritique.* Paris: Nathan.

Ducournau, Claire. 2010. "Mélancolie postcoloniale? La réception décalée du roman *Monnè, outrages et défis* d'Ahmadou Kourouma (1990)." *ARSS* 185: 82–95.

———. 2011. "From One Place to Another: The Transnational Mobility of Contemporary Francophone Sub-Saharan African Writers." *Yale French Studies* 120: 49–61.

———. 2015. "How African Literature Is Made: The Case of Authors from Francophone Sub-Saharan Africa (1960–2010)." In *Institutions of World Literature: Writing, Translation, Markets,* edited by Stefan Helgesson and Pieter Vermeulen, 160–73. New York: Routledge.

———. 2017. *La Fabrique des classiques africains. Écrivains d'Afrique subsaharienne francophone.* Paris: CRNS Éditions.

———. 2019. "African Literary Festivals and World Literature: From the Map to the Territory." *Journal of World Literature* 4, no. 2: 237–57.

———, Tristan Leperlier, and Gisèle Sapiro, eds. 2020. "La littérature au-delà des nations. Hommage à Pascale Casanova." *CoNTEXTE.*

Durand, Pascal. 2008. *Mallarmé.* Paris: Seuil.

Durkheim, Émile. 1982. *The Rules of Sociological Method.* Translated by W. D. Halls. New York: Free Press [1898].

Eagleton, Terry. 2007. *Ideology. An Introduction.* New York: Verso [1991].

———. 2008. *Literary Theory: An Introduction.* 3rd ed. Minneapolis: University of Minnesota Press.

Eco, Umberto. 1989. *The Open Work.* Translated by Anna Cancogni; introduction by David Robey. Cambridge, MA: Harvard University Press [1962].

English, James F. 2008. *The Economy of Prestige. Prizes, Awards, and the Circulation of Cultural Value.* Cambridge, MA: Harvard University Press.

Escarpit, Robert. 1958. *Sociologie de la littérature.* Paris: PUF, coll. "Que sais-je?"

———, ed. 1970. *Le Littéraire et le social.* Paris: PUF.

———. 1971. *Sociology of Literature.* Translated by Ernest Pick. London: Frank Cass Publishers.

Espagne, Michel. 1999. *Les Transferts culturels franco-allemands.* Paris: PUF.

———, and Michael Werner, eds. 1990. *Philologiques.* Paris: Éditions de la MSH.

Establet, Roger, and Georges Felouzis. 1992. *Livre et télévision. Concurrence ou intéraction?* Paris: PUF.

Even-Zohar, Itamar. 1990. "Polysystem Studies." *Poetics Today* 11, no. 1: 9–26.

Evangelista, Stefano-Maria. 2009. *British Aestheticism and Ancient Greece: Hellenism, Reception, Gods in Exile.* Basingstoke, UK: Palgrave Macmillan.

———. 2021. *Literary Cosmopolitanism in the English Fin de Siècle Citizens of Nowhere.* Oxford: Oxford University Press.

Fabiani, Jean-Louis. 2008. *L'Éducation populaire et le théâtre. Le Public d'Avignon en action.* Saint Martin d'Hères, France: Presses Universitaires de Grenoble.

———, and Fabienne Soldini. 1995. *Lire en prison.* Paris: Éditions de la BPI–Centre Georges Pompidou.

Fassin, Eric. 2001. "Le Double 'je' de Christine Angot. Sociologie du pacte littéraire." *Sociétés et Représentations* 11: 143–66.

Febvre, Lucien. 1985. *The Problem of Unbelief in the Sixteenth Century: The Religion of Rabelais.* Translated by Beatrice Gottlieb. Cambridge, MA: Harvard University Press.

Febvre, Lucien. 2014. *Le problème de l'incroyance au XVIe siècle. La religion de Rabelais*. Paris: Albin Michel [1942].

Flanders, Julia, and Fotis Jannadis, eds. 2018. *The Shape of Data in Digital Humanities: Modeling Texts and Text-Based Resources: Digital Research in the Arts and Humanities*. London: Routledge.

Fonkoua, Romuald Blaise, and Pierre Halen, eds. 2001. *Les Champs littéraires africains*. Paris: Karthala.

Fossé-Poliak, Claude, Gérard Mauger, and Bernard Pudal. 1999. *Histoire de lecteurs*. Paris: Nathan.

Foucault, Michel. 1994. "Qu'est-ce qu'un auteur?" In *Dits et écrits*, vol. 1: *1954–1988*, 789–820. Paris: Gallimard [1969].

——. 1999. "What Is An Author?" In *Aesthetics, Method, and Epistemology*, edited by J. D. Faubion, 205–22. New York: New Press.

Fraisse, Emmanuel, ed. 1993. *Les Étudiants et la lecture*. Paris: PUF.

——. 1997. *Les Anthologies en France*. Paris: PUF.

Franssen, Thomas, and Giselinde Kuipers, eds. 2015. "Sociology of Literature in the Early 21st Century: Away from the Centre," special issue, *Cultural Sociology* 9, no. 3.

Fraser, Nancy. 2007. "Transnationalizing the Public Sphere: On the Legitimacy and Efficacy of Public Opinion in a Post-Westphalian World." *Theory, Culture & Society* 24, no. 4: 7–30.

Fréché, Bibiane. 2009. *Littérature et société en Belgique francophone (1944–1960)*. Brussels: Le Cri.

Freidson, Eliot. 1986. "Les Professions artistiques comme défi à l'analyse sociologique." *Revue française de sociologie* 27, no. 3: 431–44.

Garrard, John Gordon, and Carol Garrard. 1990. *Inside the Soviet Writers' Union*. New York: Free Press.

Gauvin, Lise, and Jean-Pierre Bertrand, eds. 2003. *Littératures mineures en langue majeure*. Brussels: Pie-Peter Lang/AML Editions.

Genet, Jean-Philippe. 2002. "Analyse factorielle et construction des variables. L'origine géographique des auteurs anglais (1300–1600)." *Histoire et mesure* 17, nos. 1–2: 87–108.

Genette, Gérard. 1987. *Seuils*. Paris: Seuil.

——. 1991. *Fiction et diction*. Paris: Seuil.

——. 1993. *Fiction and Diction*. Translated by Catherine Porter. Ithaca: Cornell University Press.

——. 1997. *Paratexts: Thresholds of Interpretation*. Translated by Jane E. Lewin. Cambridge: Cambridge University Press.

Giorgi, Liana. 2009. "Literature Festivals and the Sociology of Literature." *International Journal of the Arts in Society* 4, no. 4: 317–26.

———. 2011. "Between Tradition, Vision and Imagination: The Public Sphere of Literature Festivals." In *Festivals and the Cultural Public Sphere*, edited by Gerard Delanty, Liana Giorgi, and Monica Sassatelli. London: Routledge.

Gleize, Joëlle, and Philippe Roussin. 2009. *La Bibliothèque de la Pléiade. Travail éditorial et valeur littéraire*. Paris: Éditions des Archives Contemporaines.

Glinoer, Anthony, and Vincent Laisney. 2013. *L'Âge des cénacles*. Paris: Fayard.

Gobille, Boris. 2005a. "Les Mobilisations de l'avant-garde littéraire française en mai 1968. Capital politique, capital littéraire et conjoncture de crise." *ARSS* 158: 30–53.

———. 2005b. "La Guerre de *Change* contre la 'dictature structuraliste' de *Tel Quel*. Le 'théoricisme' des avant-gardes littéraires à l'épreuve de la crise politique de Mai 68." *Raisons politiques* 18: 73–96.

———. 2018. *Le Mai 68 des écrivains. Crise politique et avant-gardes littéraires*. Paris: CNRS Éditions.

Goffman, Erving. 1974. *Frame Analysis: An Essay on the Organization of Experience*. Boston: Northeastern University Press.

Goldmann, Lucien. 1955. *Le Dieu caché. Étude sur la vision tragique dans les* Pensées *de Pascal et dans le théâtre de Racine*. Paris: Gallimard.

———. 1964. *Pour une sociologie du roman*. Paris: Gallimard.

———. 1968. "Criticism and Dogmatism in Literature." In *The Dialectics of Liberation*, edited by David Cooper. London: Penguin.

———. 1970. "Critique et dogmatisme dans la création littéraire." In *Marxisme et sciences humaines*. Paris: Gallimard.

———. 1975. *Towards a Sociology of the Novel*. London: Tavistock Publications.

———. 2016. *The Hidden God: A Study of Tragic Vision in the Pensées of Pascal and the Tragedies of Racine*. Translated by Philip Thody. London: Verso.

Goldstein, Jan. 1984. "'Moral Contagion': A Professional Ideology of Medicine and Psychiatry in Eighteenth- and Nineteenth-Century France." In *Professions and the French State, 1700–1900*, edited by Gerald L. Geison, 181–222. Philadelphia: University of Pennsylvania Press.

Griswold, Wendy. 2000. *Bearing Witness. Readers, Writers, and the Novel in Nigeria*. Princeton: Princeton University Press.

Guyau, Jean-Marie. 1887. *L'Art au point de vue sociologique*. Paris: Alcan.

Harchi, Kaoutar. 2021. "Une carte d'identité littéraire? L'Invention de l'écrivain 'beur' dans la France des années 1980." *Actes de la recherche en sciences sociales* 238, no. 3: 4–21.

Hauser, Arnold. 1982. *Histoire sociale de l'art et de la littérature*. 3 vols. Paris: Le Sycomore.

———. 1999. *The Social History of Art*, vol. 3: *Rococo, Classicism and Romanticism*. Translated by Stanley Godman. 3rd ed. London: Routledge.

Hébrard, Jean. 1990. "Les Nouveaux lecteurs." In *Histoire de l'édition française*, vol. *3*., edited by Roger Chartier and Henri-Jean Martin, 526–68. Paris: Fayard/Promodis.

Heilbron, Johan. 1995. *The Rise of Social Theory*. Cambridge, UK: Polity.

———. 1999. "Towards a Sociology of Translation: Book Translations as a Cultural World System." *European Journal of Social Theory* 2, no. 4: 429–44.

———. 2008. "L'Évolution des échanges culturels entre la France et les Pays-Bas face à l'hégémonie de l'anglais." In *Translatio. Le Marché de la traduction en France à l'heure de la mondialisation*, edited by Gisèle Sapiro, 311–32. Paris: CNRS Éditions.

———, and Gisèle Sapiro. 2015. "Translation: Economic and Sociological Perspectives." In *Palgrave Handbook of Economics and Language*, edited by Victor Ginsburgh and Shlomo Weber, 373–402. Basingstoke, UK: Palgrave Macmillan.

Heinich, Nathalie. 1999. *L'Épreuve de la grandeur*. Paris: La Découverte.

———. 2000. *Être écrivain. Création et identité*. Paris: La Découverte.

———. 2005. *L'Élite artiste. Excellence et singularité en régime démocratique*. Paris: Gallimard.

Helgesson, Stefan, and Pieter Vermeulen, eds. 2015. *Institutions of World Literature: Writing, Translation, Markets*. London: Routledge.

Hesse, Carla. 1990. "Enlightenment Epistemology and the Laws of Authorship in Revolutionary France, 1777–1793." *Representations* 30: 109–37.

Hockx, Michel. 2012. "The Literary Field and the Field of Power: The Case of Modern China." *Paragraph* 35, no. 1: 49–65.

————. 2019. *The Literary Field of Twentieth Century China*. London: Routledge [1999].

Hoggart, Richard. 2009. *The Uses of Literacy*. London: Chatto and Windus [1957].

Hollier, Denis. 1988. *The College of Sociology*. Translated by Betsy Wing. Minneapolis: University of Minnesota Press.

————. 1995. *Le Collège de sociologie*. Paris: Gallimard [1979].

Horellou-Lafarge, Chantal, and Monique Segré. 2007. *Sociologie de la lecture*. Paris: La Découverte.

Huggan, Graham. 2001. *The Postcolonial Exotic. Marketing the Margins*. London: Routledge.

Idt, Geneviève. 1979. "Modèles scolaires dans l'écriture sartrienne. *La Nausée*, ou la 'narration' impossible." *Revue des sciences humaines* 174: 83–103.

Illouz, Eva. 2014. *Hard-Core Romance: Fifty Shades of Grey, Best-Sellers, and Society*. Chicago: University of Chicago Press.

Jacquemond, Richard. 2003. *Entre scribes et écrivains. Le Champ littéraire dans l'Égypte contemporaine*. Arles, France: Actes Sud/Sinbad.

————. 2008. *Conscience of the Nation: Writers, State, and Society in Modern Egypt*. Cairo: American University in Cairo Press.

————. 2018. "Translation and Cultural Hegemony: The Case of French-Arabic Translation." In *Rethinking Translation*, edited by Lawrence Venuti, 139–58. London: Routledge [1992].

Jameson, Frederic. 1981. *The Political Unconscious: Narrative as a Socially Symbolic Act*. Ithaca: Cornell University Press.

————. *Archaeologies of the Future: The Desire Called Utopia and Other Science Fictions*. New York: Verso, 2005.

Janssen, Susanne. 1997. "Reviewing as Social Practice: Institutional Constraints on Critics' Attention for Contemporary Fiction." *Poetics* 24: 275–97.

Jauss, Hans Robert. 1982. *Toward an Aesthetic of Reception*. Translated by Timothy Bahti. Minneapolis: University of Minnesota Press.

Jeannelle, Jean-Louis. 2008. *Écrire ses mémoires au XXe siècle. Déclin et renouveau d'une tradition*. Paris: Gallimard.

Jeanpierre, Laurent. 2004. "Des hommes entre plusieurs mondes. Étude sur une situation d'exil. Intellectuels français réfugiés aux États-Unis pendant la Deuxième Guerre mondiale." PhD diss., EHESS.

Joch, Marcus, and Norbert Wolf, eds. 2005. *Text und Feld. Bourdieu in der literaturwissenchaftlichen Praxis*. Tübingen: Max Niemeyer Verlag.

Jouhaud, Christian. 2000. *Les Pouvoirs de la littérature. Histoire d'un paradoxe*. Paris: Gallimard.

Jurt, Joseph. 1980. *La Réception de la littérature par la critique journalistique. Lectures de Bernanos, 1926–1936*. Paris: J.-M. Place.

———. 1992. "Autonomie ou hétéronomie. Le Champ littéraire en France et en Allemagne." *Regards sociologiques* 4: 3–16.

Kaës, Emmanuelle. 2020. *Proust à l'école*. Geneva: Droz.

Kauppi, Niilo. 1991. *Tel Quel. La Constitution sociale d'une avant-garde*. Helsinki: Finnish Society of Sciences and Letters.

———. 2013. *The Making of an Avant-Garde: Tel Quel*. Berlin: De Gruyter Mouton [1994].

Kleppinger, Kathryn. 2016. *Branding the "Beur" Author: Minority Writing and the Media in France*. Liverpool: Liverpool University Press.

Klinkenberg, Jean-Marie. 2006. "Réseaux et trajectoires." In *Les Réseaux littéraires*, edited by Daphné De Mareneffe and Benoît Denis, 71–85. Brussels: Le Cri.

LaCapra, Dominick. 1982. *Madame Bovary on Trial*. Ithaca: Cornell University Press.

Lacouture, Jean. 1980. *François Mauriac*. Paris: Seuil.

Ladenson, Elisabeth. 2007. *Dirt for Art's Sake: Books on Trial from Madame Bovary to Lolita*. Ithaca: Cornell University Press.

Lafarge, Claude. 1983. *La Valeur littéraire. Figuration littéraire et usages sociaux des fictions*. Paris: Fayard.

Lahire, Bernard. 2006. *La Condition littéraire. La Double vie des écrivains*. Paris: La Découverte.

———. 2010a. "The Double Life of Writers." *New Literary History* 41, no. 2: 443–65.

———. 2010b. *Franz Kafka. Éléments pour une théorie de la création littéraire*. Paris: La Découverte.

Lanson, Gustave. 1904. "L'histoire littéraire et la sociologie." *Revue de métaphysique et de morale* 12: 621–42.

———. 1995. "Literary History and Sociology." Translated by Nicholas T. Rand. *PMLA* 110, no. 2: 220–35.

Leclerc, Yvan. 1991. *Crimes écrits. La Littérature en procès au 19ᵉ siècle*. Paris: Plon.

Leenhardt, Jacques, and Pierre Józsa. 1999. *Lire la lecture. Essai de sociologie de la lecture*. Paris: L'Harmattan [1982].

Lepenies, Wolf. 1988. *Between Literature and Science: The Rise of Sociology*. Cambridge: Cambridge University Press.

Leperlier, Tristan. 2018. *Algérie, les écrivains dans la décennie noire*. Paris: CNRS Éditions.

———. 2019. "On Islands and Deserts: Algerian Worlds." *Journal of World Literature* 4, no. 1: 215–36.

———. 2022. "Linguistic Areas of Literature: Between the World and the Nations." In *Pascale Casanova's World of Letters and Its Legacies*, edited by Gisèle Sapiro and Delia Ungureanu, 129–46. Leiden: Brill.

Levin, Harry. 1946. "Literature as an Institution." *Accent* no. 3: 159–68.

Lévy, Clara.1998. *Écritures de l'identité. Les Écrivains juifs après la Shoah*. Paris: PUF.

Lidsky, Paul. 1970. *Les Écrivains contre la Commune*. Paris: Maspero.

Lilti, Antoine. 2005. *Le Monde des salons. Sociabilité et mondanité à Paris au XVIIIᵉ siècle*. Paris: Fayard.

———. 2015. *The World of Salons: Sociability and Worldliness in Eighteenth-Century Paris*. Translated by Lydia G. Cochrane. Oxford: Oxford University Press.

Lough, John. 1978. *The Writer and Public in France: From the Middle Ages to the Present Day*. Oxford: Oxford University Press.

Lucey, Michael. 2003. *The Misfit of the Family: Balzac and the Social Forms of Sexuality*. Durham, NC: Duke University Press.

Lyon-Caen, Judith. 2006. *La Lecture et la vie. Les Usages du roman au temps de Balzac*. Paris: Tallandier.

———, and Dinah Ribard. 2010. *L'Historien et la littérature*. Paris: La Découverte.

Lyons, Martin. 1987. *Le Triomphe du livre. Une histoire sociologique de la lecture dans la France du XIXᵉ siècle*. Paris: Promodis/Éditions du Cercle de la Librairie.

Macherey, Pierre. 1971. *Pour une théorie de la production littéraire*. Paris: Maspero.

———. 1978. *A Theory of Literary Production*. London: Routledge and Kegan Paul.

Mackenzie, Donald. 1999. *Bibliography and the Sociology of Texts*. Cambridge: Cambridge University Press.

Maggetti, Daniel. 1995. *L'Invention de la littérature romande 1830–1910*. Paris: Payot.

Malela, Buata Bundu. 2008. *Les Écrivains afro-antillais à Paris (1920–1960). Stratégies et postures identitaires*. Paris: Karthala.

Marneffe, Daphné, and Benoît Denis, eds. "Réseaux et trajectoires." In *Les Réseaux littéraires*, 71–85. Brussels: Le Cri.

Masseau, Didier. *L'Invention de l'intellectuel au XVIIIe siècle*. Paris: PUF.

Matonti, Frédérique. 2005. *Intellectuels communistes. Essai sur l'obéissance politique. La Nouvelle Critique (1967-1980)*. Paris: La Découverte.

Mattelart, Armand, and Érik Neveu. 2008. *Introduction aux Cultural Studies*. Paris: La Découverte.

Mauger, Gérard, and Claude Poliak. 1998. "Les Usages sociaux de la lecture." *ARSS* 123: 3–24.

McDonald, Peter. 2009. *The Literature Police: Apartheid Censorship and Its Cultural Consequences*. Oxford: Oxford University Press.

McGrath, Laura. 2021. "Literary Agency." *American Literary History* 33, no. 2: 350–70.

McGurl, Mark. 2009. *The Program Era: Postwar Fiction and the Rise of Creative Writing*. Cambridge, MA: Harvard University Press.

McMartin, Jack. 2019. "A Small, Stateless Nation in the World Market for Book Translations: The Politics and Policies of the Flemish Literature Fund." *TTR: Traduction Terminologie Redaction* 32, no. 1: 145–75.

Meizoz, Jérôme. 1997. *Ramuz. Un passager clandestin des lettres françaises*. Geneva: Éditions Zoé.

———. 2001. *L'Âge du roman parlant (1919-1939). Écrivains, critiques, linguistes et pédagogues en débat*. Geneva: Droz.

———. 2003. *Le Gueux philosophe (Jean-Jacques Rousseau)*. Geneva: Antipodes.

———. 2004. *L'Œil sociologique et la littérature. Essai*. Geneva: Slatkine.

———. 2007. *Postures littéraires. Mises en scène modernes de l'auteur*. Geneva: Slatkine.

———. 2016. *La Littérature "en personne." Scène médiatique et formes d'incarnation*. Geneva: Slatkine.

———. 2020. *Faire l'auteur en régime néo-libéral. Rudiments de marketing littéraire*. Geneva: Slatkine.

Memmi, Dominique. 1998. *Jules Romains ou la passion de parvenir*. Paris: La Dispute.

Merton, Robert K. 1968. *Social Theory and Social Structure*, revised and enlarged edition. New York: Free Press.

Meyerlarts, Reine, and Diana Roig-Sanz, eds. 2018. *Literary Transla-*

tion and Cultural Mediators in "Peripheral" Cultures: Custom Offi-cers or Smugglers, 183–210. London: Palgrave Macmillan.

Miceli, Sergio. 1975. "Division du travail entre les sexes et division du travail de domination. Étude clinique des anatoliens au Brésil." *ARSS* 5–6: 162–82.

———. 1981. *Les Intellectuels et le pouvoir au Brésil (1920–1945).* Paris: Éditions de la Maison des Sciences de l'Homme.

———. 2007. "Jorge Luis Borges, histoire sociale d'un 'écrivain-né.'" *ARSS* 168: 82–101.

Miller, Christopher L. 1998. *Nationalists and Nomads. Essays on Fran-cophone African Literature*. Chicago: University of Chicago Press.

Milligan, Jennifer. 1996. *The Forgotten Generation: French Women Writers of the Interwar Period*. New York: Berg Publishers.

Milo, Daniel. 1984. "La Bourse mondiale de la traduction. Un baromètre culturel." *Annales. Économies, Sociétés, Civilisations* 1: 92–115.

Moretti, Franco. 1997. *Atlas of the European Novel 1800–1900*. New York: Verso.

———. 2000a. *The Way of the World: The Bildungsroman in European Culture*. London: Verso.

———. 2000b. "Conjectures on World Literature." *New Left Review* 1 (January–February): 1–12.

———. 2005. *Graphs, Maps, Trees: Abstract Modes for Literary History*. New York: Verso.

Moudileno, Lydie. 2000. *L'Écrivain antillais au miroir de sa littéra-ture. Mises en scène et mise en abyme du roman antillais*. Paris: Karthala.

———. 2006. *Parades postcoloniales. La Fabrication des identités dans le roman congolais*. Paris: Karthala.

Murat, Laure. 2005. "The Invention of the Neuter." *Diogenes* 52, no. 4: 61–72.

———. 2006. *La Loi du genre. Une histoire culturelle du "troisième sexe."* Paris: Fayard.

Narayanan, Pavithra. 2012. *What Are You Reading ? The Word Market and Indian Literary Production*. London: Routledge.

Naudier, Delphine. 2000. "La Cause littéraire des femmes. Mode d'ac-cès et de consécration des femmes dans le champ littéraire depuis les années 1970." PhD diss., EHESS.

———. 2001. "L'Écriture-femme, une innovation esthétique embléma-tique." *Sociétés contemporaines* 4, no. 44: 57–73.

———. 2004. "L'Irrésistible élection de Marguerite Yourcenar à l'Académie Française." *Cahiers du genre* 1, no. 36: 45–67.

Neveu, Eric. 1985. *L'Idéologie dans le roman d'espionnage.* Paris: Presses de la Fondation Nationale des Sciences Politiques.

Norris, Susan. 2006. "The Booker Prize: A Bourdieusian Perspective." *Journal for Cultural Research* 10, no. 2: 139–58.

Ommundsen, Wenche. 2009. "Literary Festivals and Cultural Consumption." *Australian Literary Studies* 24, no.1: 19–34.

Parkhurst Ferguson, Priscilla. 1987. *Literary France: The Invention of a Culture.* Berkeley: University of California Press.

Parmentier, Patrick. 1986. "Les Genres et leurs lecteurs." *Revue française de sociologie* 27, no. 3: 397–430.

Pequignot, Bruno. 2001. *La Relation amoureuse—Analyse sociologique du roman sentimental moderne.* Paris: L'Harmattan.

Péroni, Michel. 1988. *Histoire de lire. Lecture et parcours biographique.* Paris: BPI/Centre Pompidou.

Picaud, Myrtille, Jérôme Pacouret, and Gisèle Sapiro. 2020. "Mapping the Public of a Literary Festival with Multiple Correspondence Analysis: The Specificity of Literary Capital." In *Investigation of Social Space,* edited by Jörg Blasius, Frédéric Lebaron, Brigitte Le Roux, and Andreas Schmitz, 229–43. Berlin: Springer.

Pickford, Susan. 2011. "The Booker Prize and the Prix Goncourt: A Case Study of Award-Winning Novels in Translation." *Book History* 14: 221–40.

Planté, Christine. 1989. *La Petite Sœur de Balzac. Essai sur la femme auteur.* Paris: Seuil.

Poliak, Claude. 2006. *Aux frontières du champ littéraire. Sociologie des écrivains amateurs.* Paris: Economica.

Ponton, Remy. 1973. "Programme esthétique et accumulation de capital symbolique. L'Exemple du Parnasse." *Revue française de sociologie* 14, no. 2: 202–20.

———. 1975. "Naissance du roman psychologique. Capital culturel, capital social et stratégie littéraire à la fin du 19e siècle." *ARSS* 4: 66–81.

———. 1977. "Le Champ littéraire de 1865 à 1906 (recrutement des écrivains, structures des carrières et production des œuvres)." PhD diss., Université Paris V.

Popa, Ioana. 2006. "Translation Channels. A Primer on Politicised Literary Transfer." *Target: International Review of Translation Studies* 18, no. 2: 205–28.

———. 2010. *Traduire sous contraintes. Littérature et communisme (1947–1989)*. Paris: CNRS Éditions.

———. 2019. "Political Commitment and the Construction of Symbolic Recognition during the Cold War: The Impact of the 1956 Crises on International Literary Transfers." *World Literature Studies* 11, no. 1: 3–14.

Poulain, Martine, ed. 1993. *Lire en France aujourd'hui*. Paris: Cercle de la Librairie.

Privat, Jean-Marie. 1994. *Bovary Charivari. Essai d'ethnocritique*. Paris: CNRS Éditions.

Pudal, Bernard. 1994. "La Seconde réception de Nizan (1960–1990)." *Cahiers de l'IHTP* 26: 199–211.

Rabot, Cécile. 2015. *La Construction de la visibilité littéraire en bibliothèque*. Paris: Presses de l'ENSSIB.

Racine, Nicole, and Michel Trebitsch, eds. 2004. *Intellectuelles. Du genre en histoire des intellectuels*. Brussels: Éditions Complexe.

Radway, Janice A. 1984. *Reading the Romance: Women, Patriarchy, and Popular Literature*. Chapel Hill: University of North Carolina Press.

Renard, Fanny. 2011. *Les Lycéens et la lecture. Entre habitudes et sollicitations*. Rennes, France: Presses Universitaires de Rennes.

Rigot, Huguette. 1993. "Les Couvertures de livres. Approches sémiologiques et sociologiques des marques éditoriales." PhD diss., EHESS.

Robin, Régine. 1986. *Le Réalisme socialiste. Une esthétique impossible*. Paris: Payot.

———. 1992. *Socialist Realism: An Impossible Aesthetic*. Translated by Catherine Porter. Stanford: Stanford University Press.

Robine, Nicole. 2000. *Lire des livres en France des années 1930 à 2000*. Paris: Cercle de la Librairie.

Roche, Daniel. 1988. *Les Républicains des lettres. Gens de culture et Lumières au XVIIIᵉ siècle*. Paris: Fayard.

Rouanet, Henri, and Brigitte Leroux. 1993. *L'Analyse des données multidimensionnelles*. Paris: Dunod.

Roussin, Philippe. 2005. *Misère de la littérature, terreur de l'histoire. Céline et la littérature contemporaine*. Paris: Gallimard.

Rundle, Christopher. 2010. *Publishing Translations in Fascist Italy*. Oxford: Peter Lang.

———, and Kate Sturge, eds. 2010. *Translation under Fascism*. London: Palgrave Macmillan.

Said, Edward. 1978. *Orientalism*. New York: Pantheon Books.

Saint-Amand, Denis. 2012. *La Littérature à l'ombre. Sociologie du Zutisme*. Paris: Garnier.

Saint-Jacques, Denis, Jacques Lemieux, Claude Martin, and Vincent Nadeau. 1994. *Ces livres que vous avez aimés. Les Best-sellers au Québec de 1970 à aujourd'hui*. Quebec: Nuit Blanche.

Saint-Martin, Monique de. 1990. "Les 'femmes écrivains' et le champ littéraire." *ARSS* 83: 52–56.

Santana-Acuña, Álvaro. 2020. *Ascent to Glory. How One Hundred Years of Solitude Was Written and Became a Global Classic*. New York: Columbia University Press.

Sapiro, Gisèle. 1999. *La Guerre des écrivains (1940–1953)*. Paris: Fayard.

———. 2002a. "The Structure of the French Literary Field during the German Occupation (1940–1944): A Multiple Correspondence Analysis." *Poetics* 30, nos. 5–6: 387–402.

———. 2002b. "L'Importation de la littérature hébraïque en France. Entre universalisme et communautarisme." *ARSS* 144: 80–98.

———. 2003a. "The Literary Field between the State and the Market." *Poetics* 31, nos. 5–6: 441–61.

———. 2003b. "Forms of Politicization in the French Literary Field." *Theory and Society* 32: 633–52.

———. 2004. "Défense et illustration de 'l'honnête homme.' Les Hommes de lettres contre la sociologie." *ARSS* 153: 1–27.

———. 2006a. "Responsibility and Freedom: Foundations of Sartre's Concept of Intellectual Engagement." *Journal of Romance Studies* 6, nos. 1–2: 31–48.

———. 2006b. "Réseaux, institutions et champ." In *Les Réseaux littéraires*, edited by Daphné Marneffe and Benoît Denis, 44–59. Brussels: Le Cri.

———. 2006c. "Portrait of the Writer as a Traitor: The French Purge Trials (1944–1953)." *EREA, Revue d'études anglophones* 4, no. 2. Reprinted in *Right/Left/Right: Revolving Commitments, France and Britain 1929–1950*, edited by Jennifer Birkett and Stan Smith (Cambridge, UK: Cambridge Scholars Publishing, 2008), 187–204.

———. 2007a. "L'Apport du concept de champ à la sociologie de la littérature." In *Littérature et sociologie*, edited by Philippe Baudorre, Dominique Rabaté, and Dominique Viart, 61–80. Bordeaux, France: Presses Universitaires de Bordeaux.

———. 2007b. "'Je n'ai jamais appris à écrire.' Les Conditions de formation de la vocation d'écrivain." *ARSS* 168: 13–33.

———. 2007c. "The Writer's Responsibility in France: From Flaubert to Sartre." *French Politics, Culture and Society* 25, no. 1: 1–29.

———, ed. 2008. *Translatio. Le Marché de la traduction en France à l'heure de la mondialisation*. Paris: CNRS Éditions.

———. 2009a. "Modèles d'intervention politique des intellectuels. Le cas français." *ARSS* 176–77: 8–31.

———, ed. 2009b. *L'Espace intellectuel en Europe. De la formation des États-nations à la mondialisation, XIXᵉ–XXIᵉ siècle*. Paris: La Découverte.

———, ed. 2009c. *Les Contradictions de la globalisation éditoriale*. Paris: Nouveau Monde Éditions.

———. 2010a. "Globalization and Cultural Diversity in the Book Market: The Case of Translations in the US and in France." *Poetics* 38, no. 4: 419–39.

———. 2010b. "The Debate on the Writer's Responsibility in France and the United States from the 1920s to the 1950s." *International Journal of Politics, Culture and Society* 23, nos. 2–3: 69–83.

———. 2010c. "Authorship and Responsibility: The Case of Emile Zola's Commitment in the Dreyfus Affair." In *Authorship Revisited: Conceptions of Authorship around 1900 and 2000*, edited by Liesbeth Korthals Altes, Gillis Dorleijn, Ralf Grüttemeier, 1–10. Leuven: Peters.

———. 2011a. "Literature's Role in Framing Perceptions of Reality: The Example of the Second World War." In *Framing Narratives of the Second World War and Occupation in France 1939–2009: New Readings*, edited by Margaret Atack and Christopher Lloyd, 21–36. Manchester, UK: Manchester University Press.

———. 2011b. *La Responsabilité de l'écrivain. Littérature, droit et morale en France (XIXᵉ–XXIᵉ siècle)*. Paris: Seuil.

———, ed. 2012. *Traduire la littérature et les sciences humaines. Conditions et obstacles*. Paris: DEPS (Ministère de la Culture).

———. 2013a. "Droits et devoirs de la fiction littéraire en régime démocratique. Du réalisme à l'autofiction." *Fixxion. Revue critique de fiction contemporaine* 6, http://revue-critique-de-fixxion-francaise-contemporaine.org/rcffc/rt/printerFriendly/fxo6.11/740.

———. 2013b. "Autofiction, between Introspection and Testimony." In *Autofiction. Literature in France Today*, edited by Tom Bishop, Coralie Girard, and Lise Landeau. New York: Center for French Civilization and Culture, 166–80.

———. 2014. *The French Writers' War, 1940–1953*. Translated by Vanessa

Doriott Anderson and Dorrit Cohn. Durham, NC: Duke University Press.

———. 2015a. "Strategies of Importation of Foreign Literature in France in the 20th Century: The Case of Gallimard, or the Making of an International Publisher." In *Institutions of World Literature: Writing, Translation, Markets*, edited by Stefan Helgesson and Pieter Vermeulen, 143–59. London: Routledge.

———. 2015b. "The World Market of Translation in the Globalization Era: Symbolic Capital and Cultural Diversity in the Publishing Field." In *Handbook of the Sociology of Art and Culture*, edited by Laurie Hankinet and Mike Savage, 262–76. New York: Routledge.

———. 2015c. "Translation and Symbolic Capital in the Era of Globalization: French Literature in the United States." *Cultural Sociology* 9, no. 3: 320–46.

———. 2016a. "How Do Literary Texts Cross Borders (or Not)." *Journal of World Literature* 1, no. 1: 81–96.

———. 2016b. "Faulkner in France, Or How to Introduce a Peripheral Unknown Author in the Center of the World Republic of Letters." *Journal of World Literature* 1, no. 3: 391–411.

———. 2016c. "The Metamorphosis of Modes of Consecration in the Literary Field: Academies, Literary Prizes, Festivals." *Poetics* 59: 5–19.

———. 2016d. "The Legal Responsibility of the Writer between Objectivity and Subjectivity: The French Case (19th–21st Century)." In *Literary Trials. Exceptio Artis and Theories of Literature in Court*, edited by Ralf Grüttemeier, 21–47. London: Bloomsbury.

———. 2016e. "Translation and Identity: Social Trajectories of the Translators of Hebrew Literature in French." *TTR: Traduction, Terminologie, Rédaction* 26, no. 2: 59–82.

———. 2017. "The Role of Publishers in the Making of World Literature: The Case of Gallimard." *Letteratura e Letterature* 11 : 81–94.

———.2018a. *Les Écrivains et la politique en œuvre, de l'affaire Dreyfus à la guerre d'Algérie*. Paris: Seuil.

———. 2018b. "Publishing Poetry in Translation: An Inquiry into the Margins of the World Book Market." In *Sociologies of Poetry Translation: Emerging Perspectives*, edited by Jacob Blakesley, 23–42. London: Bloomsbury.

———. 2019. "The Writing Profession in France: Between Symbolic and Professional Recognition." *French Cultural Studies* 30, no. 2: 105–20.

———. 2020a. "The Transnational Literary Field between (Inter)-

Nationalism and Cosmopolitanism." *Journal of World Literature* 5, n o. 4: 481–504.

———. 2020b. *Peut-on dissocier l'oeuvre de l'auteur?* Paris: Seuil.

———. 2021. "Le champ littéraire. Penser le fait littéraire comme fait social." *Histoire de la recherche contemporaine* 10, no. 1: 45–51.

———. 2022. "Literature Festivals: A New Authority in the Transnational Literary Field." *Journal of World Literature* 7: 303–31.

———. 2023. "Literature, Knowledge and Worldview." In *The Routledge Handbook to the History and Sociology of Ideas*, edited by Stefanos Geroulanos and Gisèle Sapiro. London: Routledge.

———. In press. "The Symbolic Economy of the Nobel Prize: Its Role in the Making of World Literature." *Poetics*.

———, and Boris Gobille. 2006. "Literary Property Owners or Intellectual Workers? French Writers in Search of a Status." *Le Mouvement social* 214: 113–39.

———, and Tristan Leperlier. 2021. "Les Agents de la globalisation éditoriale. Stratégies de conquête et de résistance." *Réseaux* 39, nos. 226–27: 127–53.

———, Tristan Leperlier, and Mohamed Amine Brahimi. 2018. "What Is a Transnational Intellectual Field?" *ARSS* 224: 4–11.

———, Myrtille Picaud, Jérôme Pacouret, and Hélène Seiler. 2015. "L'Amour de la littérature. Le Festival, nouvelle instance de production de la croyance. Le Cas des Correspondances de Manosque." *Actes de la recherche en sciences sociales* 206–7: 108–37.

———, and Cécile Rabot, eds. 2017. *Profession? Écrivain*. Paris: CNRS Éditions.

———, and Delia Ungureanu, eds. 2020. "Pascale Casanova's World of Letters and Legacies." *Journal of World Literature*, 5, no. 2. Expanded edition: *Pascale Casanova's World of Letters and Its Legacies* (Leiden: Brill, 2022).

Sartre, Jean-Paul. 1955. "François Mauriac and Freedom." In *Literary and Philosophical Essays*, 7–23. New York: Criterion. Reprinted as "Monsieur Mauriac and Freedom," in *Critical Essays (Situations I)*, translated by Chris Turner (London: Seagull, 2010), 47–84.

———. 1975. *Qu'est-ce que la littérature*. Paris: Gallimard [1948].

———. 1988a. *L'Idiot de la famille*. 3 vols. Paris: Gallimard [1971–72].

———. 1988b. *What Is Literature? And Other Essays*. Translated by Steven Ungar. Cambridge, MA: Harvard University Press.

———. 1993. "M. François Mauriac et la liberté." In *Critiques littéraires (Situations I)*, 33–53. Paris: Gallimard [1939].

———. 2023. *The Idiot of the Family: Gustave Flaubert, 1821–1857.* Translated by Carol Cosman. Chicago: University of Chicago Press.

Sayre, Robert. 2011. *La Sociologie de la littérature. Histoire, problématique, synthèse critique.* Paris: L'Harmattan.

Schaeffer, Jean-Marie. 1989. *Qu'est-ce qu'un genre littéraire ?* Paris: Seuil.

———. 1999. *Pourquoi la fiction ?* Paris: Seuil.

———. 2010. *Why Fiction?* Lincoln: University of Nebraska Press.

Schildgen, Brenda, and Ralph Hexter, eds. *Reading the Past across Space and Time: Receptions and World Literature.* London: Palgrave Macmillan, 2016.

Segall, Jeffrey. 1993. *Joyce in America. Cultural Politics and the Trials of Ulysses.* Berkeley: University of California Press.

Seibel, Bernadette. 1995. *Lire, faire lire. Des usages de l'écrit aux politiques de lecture.* Paris: Le Monde Éditions.

Seigel, Jerrold. 1986. *Bohemian Paris: Culture, Politics and the Boundaries of Bourgeois Life, 1830–1930.* New York: Viking Penguin.

Serry, Hervé, ed. 2001. "Littératures et sociétés." *Sociétés contemporaines* 44.

———. 2002. "Constituer un catalogue littéraire. La Place des traductions dans l'histoire des Éditions du Seuil." *ARSS* 144: 70–79.

———. 2004. *Naissance de l'intellectuel catholique.* Paris: La Découverte.

Shücking, Levin L. 1966. *The Sociology of Literary Taste.* London: Routledge and Kegan Paul [1931].

Sorá, Gustavo. 2002. "Un échange dénié. La Traduction d'auteurs brésiliens en Argentine." *ARSS* 145: 61–70.

Speller, John R. W. 2011. *Bourdieu and Literature.* Open Book Publishers. https://www.openbookpublishers.com/books/10.11647/obp.0027.

Spivak, Gayatri. 1987. *In Other Worlds: Essays in Cultural Politics.* New York: Methuen.

———. 1988. "Can the Subaltern Speak?" In *Marxism and Interpretation of Culture,* edited by Cary Nelson and Lawrence Grossberg, 271–313. Urbana: University of Illinois Press.

Staël, Germaine de. 1991. *De la littérature considérée dans ses rapports avec les institutions sociales.* Paris: Flammarion.

———. 2000. *Literature Considered in Its Relation to Social Institutions.* Translated by Morris Berger. New York: Routledge.

Suleiman, Susan. 1983. *Authoritarian Fictions: The Ideological Novel as a Literary Genre.* Princeton: Princeton University Press.

Taine, Hippolyte. 1871. *History of English Literature*. Translated by H. Van Laun. New York: Holt and Williams.

——. 1885–87. *Histoire de la littérature anglaise*. Paris: Hachette [1864].

Thérenty, Marie-Ève. 2007. *La Littérature au quotidien. Poétiques journalistiques au XIXe siècle*. Paris: Seuil.

Thiesse, Anne-Marie. 1980. "L'Éducation sociale d'un romancier. Le cas d'Eugène Sue." *ARSS* 32–33: 51–64.

——. 1984. *Le Roman du quotidien. Lecteurs et lectures populaires à la Belle Époque*. Paris: Le Chemin Vert.

——.1991. *Écrire la France. Le Mouvement régionaliste de langue française entre la Belle Époque et la Libération*. Paris: PUF.

——. 1999. *La Création des identités nationales: Europe XVIIIᵉ-XIXᵉ siècles*. Paris: Seuil.

——. 2020. *La Fabrique de l'écrivain national. Entre littérature et politique*. Paris: Gallimard.

——. 2022. *The Creation of National Identities: Europe 18th–20th Centuries*. Translated by Brian McNeil. Leiden: Brill.

——, and Hélène Mathieu. 1981. "Déclin de l'âge classique et naissance des classiques. L'Évolution des programmes littéraires de l'agrégation depuis 1890." *Littérature* 42: 89–108.

Thomas, Dominic. 2006. *Black France: Colonialism, Immigration, and Transnationalism*. Bloomington: Indiana University Press.

Thompson, John B. 2010. *Merchants of Culture. The Publishing Business in the Twenty-First Century*. Cambridge, UK: Polity Press.

Thumerel, Fabrice. 2002. *Le Champ littéraire français au XXᵉ siècle. Éléments pour une sociologie de la littérature*. Paris: Armand Colin.

——, ed. 2004. *Annie Ernaux, une œuvre de l'entre-deux*. Arras, France: Artois Presses Université.

Tocqueville Alexis de. 1967. *L'Ancien Régime et la Révolution*. Paris: Gallimard [1856].

——. 2008. *The Ancien Régime and the Revolution*. Translated by Gerald Bevan. London: Penguin [1856].

Todd, Richard. 1996. *Consuming Fictions: The Booker Prize and Fiction in Britain Today*. London: Bloomsbury.

Todorov, Tzvetan, ed. 2001. *Théorie de la littérature. Textes des formalistes russes*. Paris: Seuil [1965].

Tommek, Heribert. 2015. *Der lange Weg in die Gegenwartsliteratur. Studien zur Geschichte des literarischen Feldes in Deutschland von 1960 bis 2000*. Berlin: De Gruyter.

——, and Klaus-Michael Bogdal, eds. 2012. *Transformationen des literarischen Feldes in der Gegenwart: Sozialstruktur, Medien-Okonomien, Autorpositionen.* Heidelberg: Synchron.

Toury, Gideon. 1995. *Descriptive Translation Studies and Beyond.* Amsterdam: John Benjamins.

Underwood, Ted. 2019. *Distant Horizons: Digital Evidence and Literary Change.* Berkeley: University of California Press.

Van Rees, Kees, and Jeroen Vermunt. 1996. "Event History Analysis of Authors' Reputation: Effects of Critics' Attention on Debutants' Careers." *Poetics* 23: 317–33.

Venuti, Lawrence. 1998. *The Scandals of Translation: Towards an Ethics of Difference.* London: Routledge.

Vessillier-Ressi, Michèle. 1982. *Le Métier d'auteur. Comment vivent-ils?* Paris: Dunod.

Viala, Alain. 1985. *Naissance de l'écrivain. Sociologie de la littérature à l'âge classique.* Paris: Minuit.

——. 1988. "Effets de champ, effets de prisme." *Littérature* 70: 64–72.

——. 1993. *Qu'est-ce qu'un classique?* Paris: Klincksieck.

——, and Georges Molinié. 1993. *Approches de la réception. Sociopoétique et sémiostylistique de Le Clézio.* Paris: PUF.

Weber, Millicent. 2018. *Literary Festivals and Contemporary Book Culture.* Palgrave Macmillan.

Wilfert-Portal, Blaise. 2002. "Cosmopolis et l'homme invisible." *ARSS* 144: 33–46.

——. 2008. "La Place de la littérature étrangère dans le champ littéraire français autour de 1900." *Art et mesure* 23, no. 2: 69–102.

Williams, Raymond. 1965. *The Long Revolution.* Harmondsworth, UK: Penguin Books [1961].

——. 1974. "On High and Popular Culture." *New Republic* 171, no. 21: 15.

——. 1977. *Marxism and Literature.* New York: Oxford University Press.

——. 1981. *Culture.* Glasgow: Fontana Press.

——. 1983. *Culture and Society.* New York: Columbia University Press [1958].

Wolf, Nelly. 1995. *Une Littérature sans histoire. Essai sur le nouveau roman.* Geneva: Droz.

——. 2005. "Le Roman comme démocratie." *Revue d'histoire littéraire de la France* 2: 343–52.

——. 2019. *Le Peuple à l'écrit. De Flaubert à Virginie Despentes.* Vincennes, France: Presses de l'Université de Vincennes.

———. 2023. *Le Juif imaginé*. Paris: CNRS Éditions.

Write Back. 2013. *Postcolonial Studies modes d'emploi*. Lyon, France: Presses Universitaires de Lyon.

Xavier, Subha. 2016. *The Migrant Text. Making and Marketing a Global French Literature*. Montreal: McGill-Queen's University Press.

Zepp, Susanne, Fine, Ruth, Gordinsky, Natasha, Konuk, Kader, Olk, Claudia and Shahar, Galili, eds. 2020. *Disseminating Jewish Literatures: Knowledge, Research, Curricula*. Berlin: De Gruyter.

Zima, Pierre V. 1985. *Manuel de sociocritique*. Paris: Picard.

Index

Page numbers in italics denote figures, and endnotes are indicated by "n" followed by the endnote number.

Printed and bound by CPI Group (UK) Ltd, Croydon, CR0 4YY

25/03/2025

14647334-0002